Praise for
How To Dump Your Wife
By Lee Covington

"You've got to read this incredible book. When I read it, I
thought the author was a guy. I said, 'Man, this guy knows how
to talk to other guys.'" —*Howard Stern*

"In chapters with headings like "Breaking the News,"
"Prepare to Unload," "Were You Trapped?," "With or Without a
Girlfriend," and "Begging and Pleading," this book breezily cov-
ers all the basics." —*The Seattle Times*

"… tells the ins and outs of how to hide your money in tax
havens overseas, with humor, of course."
  —*The New Orleans Times-Picayune*

" … a book about men and women in which men are not
automatically the villains." —*The Flint Journal*

"The book is not to encourage families to break up, but is
more of a warning – or a combat manual, if you will –
on what to expect and prepare for, legally, financially and
otherwise." —*The Sunday Oregonian*

"The finest preventive medicine on the market. I recommend
a strong dose of this book to any man wanting out of a bad marriage." —*Dr. Jerome Cox, psychiatrist*

"Right on target about my wife!" —*Anonymous, finally free!*

Also From KickAssMedia

www.kickassmedia.com

The *How to Dump Your Wife* Audio Book

Kick Ass in College

The *Kick Ass in College* Audio Book

Coming Soon From KickAssMedia

Kick Ass at Work

The *Kick Ass at Work* Audio Book

How to
DUMP
Your Wife
Practical advice
for the good man
trapped in a
bad marriage

LEE COVINGTON

DALLAS, TEXAS • BANGKOK, THAILAND

HOW TO DUMP YOUR WIFE:
PRACTICAL ADVICE FOR THE GOOD MAN TRAPPED IN A BAD MARRIAGE

Copyright © 2005 by L. Covington.

Paperback editions: September 1996, January 2005, Hardcover edition: 1994.
All rights reserved under International and Pan-American Copyright Conventions.
Published in the United States by KickAssMedia, 12358 Coit Road, PMB #317, Dallas, Texas 75251-2308.

Edited by Dr. Gary Wunderlicht
Cover design and illustrations by Scott Reed, www.websbestdesigns.com
Grateful acknowledgement is made to the American Bar Association for permission to reprint the tables that appear in the Appendix. From *Family Law in the 50 States*, published by the Family Law Section of the American Bar Association. Copyright © 2004–2005 American Bar Association.

The publisher also wishes to thank Howard Stern and *The Howard Stern Show* for their support. Free Howard and FCCK the FCC.

No portion of this book may be reproduced or transmitted in any form except brief extracts for the purpose of review, without written permission from the publisher.

ISBN 0-9762928-0-7   SAN 256 - 3061
Library of Congress Catalog Card Number 94-070591
Publisher's Cataloging-in Publication

Covington, Lee.
    How to dump your wife / by Lee Covington. -- Dallas, Texas : KickAssMedia, 2005, c1994. p. ;
cm.
Originally published: Seattle, Wash. : Fender Pub. Co., ©1994.
Includes bibliographical references and index.
    ISBN: 0-9762928-0-7 (pbk.)
    1. Divorce--United States. 2. Divorce--United States--Psychological aspects. 3. Divorce settlements--United States.
I. Title.
    HQ834 .C66 2005
    306.89/0973--dc22 0501   2004116304
KickAssMedia (www.kickassmedia.com) is a division of Nana Plaza, LLC, Dallas, Texas and Bangkok, Thailand.

To order additional copies visit **www.kickassmedia.com**, refer to the order form in back of book, or call **1-877-MY-COOL-BOOK (1-877-692-6652)**

To collect your FREE gift worth $75 send an email to
gift@howtodumpyourwife.com

This book is dedicated to all the men who have lost it all — their kids, their careers, their reputations, their freedom, even their lives. Because of a wife.

IMPORTANT
THIS BOOK IS FOR ENTERTAINMENT PURPOSES ONLY.

KICKASSMEDIA
publisher@kickassmedia.com

CONTENTS

A woman always has her revenge ready.
                                    —Molière

Introduction

Your Emancipation Proclamation

Whenever they hear the words "Family Values," capital F, capital V, some men – very few – heave a big sigh of relief.

Two kinds of men do this.

The first kind: The lucky ones who have wives from heaven, dream wives. She's the woman you've always been searching for, wouldn't give up for a million dollars. Other men wish they had her; she's not like other women at all. No, she's unique, she's beautiful, she's perfect in her own way, she's … just like you. (Sigh.)

The second kind: The ones who wouldn't dump anything, even a bag of garbage. Dump the wife? God forbid! You had to beg her to marry you in the first place. She may be average-looking, but she's the best you could do. At least, she showed up at the wedding. What would you do without her? She's holding you together at the seams. Just pray that you die first. Thank God for Family Values. (Sigh.)

This book is for the *rest* of mankind.

If you're Mister Lucky or Mister Dependent, above, and you bought the book out of curiosity, enjoy it. But remember, this is a user's manual written for those who bought it for a different reason. These are the ones who have been thinking about dumping their wives for a long time or only for a few minutes. This is a manual for serious readers. You have your reasons. Before you make some important decisions, you want some frank advice about how to dump your wife. Chances are it'll be your first and – let's hope – your last time.

There are two kinds of chapters in this book. The chapters listed under *Nuts And Bolts* will give you practical advice before, during, and after the big heave-ho. The chapters called *In Your Mind* will help you get over the hurdles that could trip you up mentally or emotionally.

Most men who want to dump their wives make a lot of the same mistakes. There's a definite tendency to flee, to simply race out the door with nothing but the shirt on your back. There's a tendency to act before you have your act together. You might be thinking that your old college buddy who went to law school will be right at your side, helping you out with all kinds of good advice. Or that your friends will be there for you, listening to your side of things and giving you the benefit of the doubt. Maybe you think your wife will somehow want to consider the future in a rational way and preserve some of your assets for herself and the children. All kinds of wild and crazy thoughts like these can cause men to commit grave mistakes. This book will help you avoid the serious errors that most men make when they dump their wives. You might even be able to save your relationship with your kids or, at least, salvage your career.

In other words, this book will help you plan things out, think things through, and get ready so that when you get free you're really free.

So take heart. You've taken the first step towards emancipation. You're going to get out. You're going to start enjoying your life. You're going to get another chance … *you're going to dump your wife.*

We'll talk about the kids. We'll talk about the lawyers. But first let's talk about the pressure. You're about to pass from the land of the good guys with Family Values into the land of the scumbags, the tramps, the jerks who are making this whole country fall apart. How could you? Get ready.

You might say to yourself, "Who cares what people think? To hell with them. They don't know me. I'm not going to live my life according to what other people think." You could say this and you're right! To hell with them if they don't like it. But get ready. It still stings when your little kid's teacher shakes her head and says, "Poor Timmy." She really means "How could you? You disgusting scumbag, you make me sick, you deserve to die."

When a woman gets out of a bad marriage, what does she get? Applause! Cheers, flowers, congratulations. Everyone is so proud of her for taking charge of her life and getting away from that awful beast. Friends throw parties, support groups gush all over her, self-esteem oozes from her pores.

But what happens when a man decides to leave his wife? Just the opposite! Everyone rushes to the wife's side. Overnight, a nice guy becomes a creep, a cheat, a crook. Judges punish you, friends desert you, the world condemns you.

It doesn't matter if your wife was the world's worst woman – unbearable and loathsome. It simply doesn't matter. It's like this: When a woman wants out, she's good; when a man wants out, he's bad.

Perhaps this is so because women have decided to award themselves the grand prize of Officially Oppressed Minority. They can do no wrong. How convenient. A minority/victim/multicultural individual cannot be criticized in any way. But even if we accept this baloney, the facts don't add up. Women are *not* in the minority and some bad women do exist. Even so, let's put reality aside for a moment and consider the trend. No one cares about your side. The rule is this: You're the bad guy because you're the man.

Believe it or not, your lawyer will be your worst moral critic – after you pay him, of course. At first you'll hear, "Oh, I understand." Then fork over the fee and it'll be, "Whaddya mean, you don't have enough money? You gonna let your poor wife starve?" Never mind that you're already paying her more than you've ever made in your life. Your own lawyer will beat you up more than anyone.

A few fallacies are coursing through this country's general mentality these days. You might have noticed that some people are looking back on the Salem witch burnings with genuine longing. So-called pro-family groups would have divorce be declared illegal. How insightful. Forced copulation.

Haven't you heard that the U.S. has the highest divorce rate in the world? Sure, you've probably heard that. It's really hard to get a divorce in France or Japan, and it's practically impossible in Ireland. So people stay married, and men have mistresses and second families. Is this what the pro-family pundits want? Is this what the feminists want? Who wants this? In Ireland the government had to change the probate laws because so many men had second "wives" and second sets of children. In France the mistresses are called "little wives."

Just watch the women here when divorce laws are stiffened and they start noticing the little wives in their lives. Or see them shiver when they really learn about sisterhood by sharing their husbands with his other family.

Our divorce rate is a measure of our civilization and progress. No talking head on TV is going to make human beings get along with each other better than they do. No amount of political pressure or "pro-family" propaganda is going to make people who can't stand each other stay together. Marrying the wrong person is a very common mistake. Fifty percent of the people who get married pick the wrong person. Why should they be forced to sacrifice their lives because of that one mistake? If the marriage doesn't work, all right, face it. Get out of it and get on with your life. If we go backwards and force people to stay together, who really gets hurt? That's right, the kids. At least divorced parents have a chance to meet the right person the next time around. It doesn't take a PhD in Parent Studies to figure out that kids are better off when their parents are happy.

It's almost time, in this country, for some original thought on this subject. But not yet. We're still soaked by lawyers who live off of our misery. We're still forced to pay people when we break their little hearts. Have you noticed how the American courts like to award vast sums of money to those who manage to have sex with rich people? If you have sex with someone who has money, you get to sue and collect big bucks! This is called "maintenance" these days, but the name of the pay-off changes from time to time. Maybe we should call it the sex partner lottery. I heard about one lawyer who finds pretty, impoverished women and introduces them to football players. When one of the girls gets pregnant, the lawyer sues the player for paternity and collects a big fee.

Why do we tolerate this sort of legal prostitution while we refuse to legalize the world's oldest profession?

Hey, no one likes a broken heart. Kind of scary. In the next century, when we get over this fear of losing our "love shelter," I believe that child support will be the only court-ordered payment in a divorce. We won't be forced to pay off a person we don't love any more. People (including women!) will begin to pay their own way. That would be nice – and fair. Adults need not support other capable adults just because they've been jilted. We can take it now, can't we? Let's get heartbreak and love out of the hands of lawyers. Let's give the money to the kids.

Then when we call a halt to the grim world of brush-off/pay-off, we can say, freedom is really freedom. Release the prisoner from the marriage cell!

That would be great. But for now the lock is still on the door. It's tough. It's rough. *But you can get away from her if you really want to*. At great cost. With great effort. No one can force you (yet) to live with and stay married to a woman you don't want. Escape is escape. If you really want a divorce, getting it will be worth the effort, no matter what other people think or say.

When people talk about Family Values, they talk about their own insecure relationships. They talk about the freedom they don't have. Or they go on and on about the small number of people who actually married the right person and live in a happy marriage. They talk about fear. Suffocation. Fantasy. Read their lips, man. They're saying, "Stay together and suffer like US."

Family Values look good on paper. Any bumpkin can write an essay about them for the Sunday editorials. They're good for vote-getting during reactionary political campaigns. They're nice when the relatives come over on holidays. But hey, Family Values aren't working for you, are they? They're not putting a muzzle on that mouth that never stops or getting that log to roll over in bed, as if you even want it to anymore … Family Values are for the guys up there, Mister Lucky and Mister Dependent. Those guys are getting something out of them. You're not.

Maybe it's time to break out. So do something. Jump back on that plane of life without all the extra baggage. Look, you bought the book. You know you want to do it. You've wasted enough time with that woman. Say it loud, say it proud: "***It's time to dump my wife***."

Chapter One

Think Back. Were You Trapped?

You're going to be very busy now. You've got a lot of thinking to do, first of all. Even before the practical nuts and bolts of getting out begin, you've got to get your head straight. So maybe you like to think hard while you're driving around or working out or just staring into space. Whatever you do. You're not part of a team anymore, man. You're on your own.

First, the relationship and the wedding. Did you really want to do it? Was your heart in it? Or did you kind of go along, figuring what the hell, it was bound to happen someday? Maybe she was really great when you first met. She was great-looking and sweet and sexy. Then, she changed. Bummer. Gradually, that honey you loved with all your heart turned into a bore. Or maybe you sort of dream-walked through the wedding because you had some other things on your mind – like your future earnings, for example. Maybe you got sick of all those subtle hints. Might as well get it over with. March down the aisle. The whole bit. I guess I owe it to her after three years of steady sex … Maybe you just wanted a couple of kids in your life, and here was someone ready to deliver the goods. Maybe, maybe everyone else seemed to be getting married, and you didn't want to be one of those older bald guys scratching around for a wife under the rocks. God … Who the hell knows? Anything could have happened.

Everyone has his own story. But there's always one thing in common: You did it, whether you wanted to or not; you let it happen.

So why get out now? You've probably learned how to make the best of your situation. Distractions such as work, friends, sports, or girlfriends can keep you on an even keel for years. You can tune her out if she really grates on you. Or you can make sure there are lots of people around when you go out together if she bores the hell out of you. You can keep on tolerating her because you've been doing it for a while, haven't you? Maybe you really do love her, but you're sick of the fighting, the mind games, the constant complaining. Sure, you can keep on tolerating your wife, but in the meantime your life is passing by.

Well, if you can tolerate your wife, maybe you better wait until your kids grow up, right? Beware of this trap. You're a miserable scumbag if you leave while they're young, but if you wait until they grow up, you'll be punished severely for the length of the marriage. No one is going to give you brownie points for sticking around. Least of all, your kids. And you'll pay thousands of dollars more for a long marriage than you will for a shorter one. I guess the lawyers feel that the longer you've suffered the more you should pay. That sounds like lawyer logic to me.[1]

---

[1] If you live in California, for example, and the marriage lasts for ten years or longer, you may automatically owe your wife *permanent* "maintenance."

But beware. It is a trap. After all, it takes quite a while for kids to grow up. That's ten, twelve, fifteen years of your life. We'll talk about kids and what to do about them in Chapter Six. So skip to that chapter if you're thinking of staying because of the kids.

Then, maybe you can find a girlfriend to fill in your lunch hours with good sex. You can stay married and still have a good time. Many men do this, but those are not men who want to dump their wives. Those men, for whatever reasons, want to stay married. Yes, it's cheaper and easier. But ask yourself this: Do you feel funny when you see a couple of people who are really in love and really together? How come they can have it and not you? Why do you have to sneak around? Or settle for a woman who only wants a married man? Obviously, she doesn't take you seriously. Or maybe she's a lot like your wife, and she wants to be married to you, or just married period. Marriage is not the object here. You've got that already. Are you a romantic at heart? Love is the object. You see it in the old movies. You read about it in books. You know it's out there, and you want to feel it sometime before you die.

Let's say you have her already. Wow. She's the girlfriend of your dreams. You want her to be your wife forever. You just want to know how to dump the old one so you can marry this one.

Or maybe you've had enough of girlfriends, wives everyone. You just want to be left alone so you can do your own thing minus the constant harassment.

If you haven't found your reason for wanting out of the marriage in this chapter, don't worry. These are only a few typical examples. No one can know how things are for you but you. Don't try to talk it out with friends – your so-called friends (see Chapter Eleven). Think about it. However you decide things, on impulse or after a long careful process, you've got to do the thinking first. Before you go on to Chapter Two, be sure that you know why you want to dump your wife. The reason isn't important, as long as you know what it is.

Take this short quiz to help yourself figure out whether or not you're serious.

1. As you read this book, do you feel queasy, excited, energized, and truly terrified?

2. Or do you feel sad, depressed, lonely, hopeless, insanely jealous of the readers who will actually be using this book?

3. Do you know, deep down, that you'd never leave your wife, but you want to torture her anyway, just to entertain yourself?

4. Do you leave this book lying around where you know she'll find it?

5. Do you have the guts to do things that you know will be incredibly difficult, because at the core you are a brave person?

6. Did you know, without admitting it, that your mother was always right about your wife?

7. Do you love your girlfriend more than life itself? Are you prepared to go through all kinds of hell just to be together?

8. Is your girlfriend aware that you'll be broke, in pain over your kids, distracted by the lawyers, and dependent on her for your emotional well-being day in and day out?

9. Can you stand to lose friends, suffer your children's anger, pay for two households, and possibly start your career all over again from scratch?

10. **The big one**: Can you imagine spending the rest of your life with that woman, your wife?

Don't kill yourself! Go on to Chapter Two.

Chapter Two

First Things First

Know this: Every married woman's biggest fear is that her husband will leave her. Biggest fear. That's bigger than the fear of poverty or the death of a child or even her own death. That's right. A child's death is much more tragic, obviously. But it's also rare. Few women run around scared to death every day that their children will suddenly drop dead. But their friends are getting dumped by their husbands right and left! Marriages are breaking up all over the place. Husbands are walking out. It's fifty percent out there. Yes, a wife is much more fearful of something that's happening all around her all the time.

So remember: Her biggest fear is that her husband will leave her. Know this and never forget it.

She is, therefore, a suspicious creature. After all, she knows that you're not madly in love with her. You're not exactly an active volcano of affection, erupting with declarations of adoration, are you?

I knew one guy whose wife used to buy her own birthday cards for herself and make him sign them. Sounds pathetic, right? This guy divorced her and later found a woman who cared as little about birthdays as he did. But don't you know, those cards, with all their flowery declarations of true love, turned up again later … in court. Wives work hard to deceive themselves when their marriages go bad. And they're like elephants. They never forget. One little whiff of the wrong perfume and she hits the roof! Different wives react in different ways.

Your wife may be living in a dream world, convinced by your once-a-year romantic outbursts that you're just one of those guys who doesn't feel comfortable expressing those feelings. She's so wrapped up in the kids and her own job or her own life that she doesn't really notice that you're ignoring her. Don't be naive. She knows something is missing. This is the ostrich type, though. Sticks her head in the sand and pretends that she doesn't know you're miles and miles away. Long as you come home every night, you're still the hero. We'll call her **Wife One**.

If this is your wife, you're lucky because she probably hasn't taken many steps to guard against your departure, even if she is aware on some subconscious Lamaze-like level. Nevertheless, she is easily influenced by her friends, daytime talk shows, and countless other sources of paranoia. You never know. Assume the worst. Watch out.

Your wife, on the other hand, might be the crafty conniving peasant-type species that has survived over the centuries by duping and trapping men and then building barbed-wire financial fences around them. Kept in a pen like a pig, are you? Have you heard this before: If you ever try to divorce me, I'll ruin you! I'll call the IRS! I'll tear your children from you forever. You'll never do [insert your business or profession here] in this town again! Sound familiar? If this tape has played in your house, even once, you can be sure she's got one or two secret bank accounts. Your money has been saved for a rainy day, the day she strolls into a lawyer's office and plunks down her first retainer. You think you keep track of your money? Guess again. This type of wife has her ways. We'll call her **Wife Two**.

Or maybe your wife is a high-powered career woman in her own right with her own assets and her own fat salary. She's a yuppie with a big job and a bigger ego. A feminist with an agenda. Beware. This woman can fight you nut for nut, bolt for bolt. Here's a modern woman with the power of ideology behind her. Maybe she's a doctor, a writer, a lawyer, a judge. Maybe she's a banker, a broker, a shrink! Whatever she is, she's hip to the system. She's connected.

And your friends? They're her friends now. You're the bad guy, remember? Everything from the pasta maker to the sleigh bed is a war treasure worth dying for, and you don't walk away from a woman like this without taking your share, right? Only partly right. It's true, you might end up with a painting or a little chest of drawers. It was fun to buy things together at first. But now, if you really want any of those treasures, you're going to have to fight for them and FIGHT is the operative word here. This woman won't be bounced out without a battle. She'll pour herself into it, in a very professional way. She's **Wife Three**.

One thing that these wives and all the other wives not featured here have in common is the fear of being dumped. No matter what they have going for them, what careers they have, what acts they try to get together, when you leave them they become dumped wives. Ninety-nine percent of them will never get over it. Whatever labels they attach to them-selves later on as they get older, there will always be one par-ticular label branded on their foreheads forever: I'm a man-hating, dumped wife. Watch out. Today. Tomorrow. Once a dumped wife, always a dumped wife. Whoa. *C'est la vie,* sister.

Let's get back to work. What's your first order of busi-ness? Look around. Begin to make mental notes. First, con-sider your business. How much does she know? Whom does she know? What could she do in the way of massive destruction? Where do you stand financially? Tax-wise? Pension? Got a 401K? Any investments? Are the assets joint or separate? Is your pension governed by ERISA? If it is, you'll need her signature to get at your money. Check it out. Is she a joint owner of your company? Or even an officer? (Big mistake. Why do we do this kind of thing to ourselves?) Is your wife connected to your professional asso-ciates by her own profession? Does she come to your office a lot? Call frequently? Know your clients?

Start thinking. Don't write anything down yet! Walk into work tomorrow and take a mental inventory. How are your records? What is your net worth? If you have to put it all on your computer to figure it out, for godssakes, don't save it!

Then do the same thing at home. Don't write anything down. And don't tell anyone, even your best friend. Just look around. Is the house or the apartment jointly owned? What's left on the mortgage? Where are most of your things? Your skis, your records, your high school football trophies? What's in your garage or the storage area? Would you be able to write it down from memory? What's the furniture worth? Did you inherit any silver or jewelry from your mom? Is there any art? The car or cars, are they in your name? What about the car insurance? What are your cars worth? What's your house worth?

Now, take a good look at what she has. How much jewelry? Fur coats? Computers? Any expensive cameras? Antiques? Can you estimate the value of her wardrobe? Take a good hard look around.

Then go somewhere private, like an outhouse in the middle of the Amish country, and write down as much as you can. Then go to a bank (not your regular one) and open your own safety deposit box and put your notes in there. Your business notes, too. Don't leave those in your office. Then hide the key to your new box as well as you can, at your office or in your locker at the gym or something. Not in your underwear drawer, you know? It's not that you're dumb, it's just that you're not used to it yet … being the enemy and being on your own.

You'll get accustomed to it soon enough. It's kind of fun. Start getting used to some new habits now. Ask yourself, Am I a credit-card creature? What about my cellular phone? My calling cards? Is my every waking moment recorded in some database? For most people, the answer is yes. It's hard to avoid being recorded these days. Now, just imagine a gradual withdrawal from this marked existence. The first step is to notice that your every step is recorded. Of course, if you have a girlfriend or two, you're already hip to the game. But if it's your first time out, you'll need to change your habits.

Don't cancel all your plastic at once! Go slowly, carefully. Use your plastic for your wife and kids. Call them from your car. But always use cash when you're alone or with a business associate or anyone else you want to keep off of the information highway. Because, now more than ever, your life is changing. I hate to tell you this, buddy, but you ain't gettin' on that information highway for a long time. You're going on your own private back road, in another direction, off on your own.

Oh, for you guys who have been sneaking around for a while already, don't relax too much. You might have your separate cards and phone already set up, but it's another ball game when the lawyers hit the field. Just watch out, more than ever before. Bank statements, credit card records, and phone records are juicy appetizers for hungry lawyers.

So guard your privacy. There's no need to go off the deep end right now and start pulling out wads of cash in a money clip or anything. Try to get onto a level of moderate paranoia. Don't talk about yourself or your plans. Watch out for paper trails.

Remember, she's a suspicious creature already. She's watching your eyes. You are starting to stir up her greatest fear and she can probably smell your desire for freedom from across the room. Watch out. Don't give her any clues. Don't stir up any trouble. I mean, be careful man. You're going to need a lot of time before she blows.

Chapter Three

Hello & Goodbye Guilt

We have to devote a whole chapter to the subject of guilt. In Chapter One you figured out why you want to do this and, more importantly, whether or not you really *will* do it. If you have a twinge or two about your reasons for wanting out, perhaps this chapter will help.

Maybe you just can't stand her anymore. You're sick of her. The sound of her voice makes you want to move to India. These are valid reasons. You're entitled to enjoy the company of the person who shares your bed. Still, though, you can't help feeling a little guilty for running out on her. Geez.

I used to say that guilt wasn't a big deal for me. I used to brag about it – like, it's a useless emotion, gets you nowhere, has no benefit. Why feel it? Now I know why. *Because I can't help it!* I'm a slave. I was born with guilt. Hand-wringing, face-wincing guilt.

Guilt is two things. It is your wife's most valuable and powerful weapon. And it is a real thing inside your head. If it were only in her hands and aimed at you, it wouldn't be nearly as dangerous. But it's in your head too, festering, and it can attack from the inside.

Maybe I should just stick it out, you say. You didn't make this marriage in a day, and you don't have to end it in a day. Take your time. You may be on the brink of disaster. After all, society won't back you up. Nor will the law. You might lose your kids. Your career. Your entire net worth. What does this have to do with guilt? If it's in you, like a parasite eating your guts, then all this other stuff – total ruination – will be much more difficult to handle.

For example, maybe you really loved your wife at one time. You promised to take care of her and protect her and all that manly stuff. You felt like a big cheese. She needed you, and you did love her. But then things changed, as they often do. You got sick of her and *bang!* Someone much better came along. So your wife is completely in the dark and thinks she's still your koochie koo or whatever. Meantime, you're onto the new one in a big way. Your girlfriend knows the real you. She's now. Wife is yesterday. But you can't help feeling bad. After all, she did hang in there when your career was careening. She maybe had a kid or two. She tried, she really did. And the saddest part is she doesn't look that good any more, and she probably won't find anyone else. Poor wife. You don't want to hurt her; you just want to get rid of her. Is the guilt coming from your old feelings about your wife? The things you once said to her? All the promises you made? All the sucking up you did with her family? Where is the guilt coming from?

It could be true that your wife is still as wonderful as she ever was – still slim, still cute, still the original sweetums. Then what's going on? You ask yourself, Why do I long for

Linda, the lady at the office? Or Kate, the cutie at the tennis court? Why? Why doesn't my still-terrific wife turn me on? What's wrong with me? *Guilt.* It's all my fault. I should stay with her, but I just want out.

Where is the guilt coming from? Your quest for freedom might not be because of your wife. Maybe she's a great gal, and you wish you could take her with you, but you can't. Sorry. And if you don't give her a good reason for leaving, she'll think one up herself. There are bunches of shrinks and friends and counselors out there ready to psychoanalyze you for her.

It's easy to imagine them. A mid-life crisis! He couldn't commit. His mother loved him too much or not enough. He's blocked. He's selfish. He's brutal … It goes on down from there. Either you know the drill already or you can see it coming.

Once the world starts giving you hell for leaving your wife, your guilt will go away by itself … to be replaced by anger, disgust, and ultimately relief.

But right now you've got it in spades. What to do about it?

A big source of guilt is any human being created by your sperm, looking up at you with big eyes, calling you daddy. Big-time guilt. You can't dismiss little Joey or adorable Zoey with some paltry excuse about wanting to live your life. Is your guilt coming from your kids? It might even be hard to separate guilt-from-wife and guilt-from-kids at this point. Try. Are they one bag of beans? The Family? Or would you really like to give your wife a big kick in the ass and let her see the Grand Canyon on her own … on the way down? Maybe you'd like to keep your kids and embark on a wild and crazy (torturous and expensive) custody battle? Maybe, bear with me, you just don't connect to your kids that much anymore. You want to fulfill your responsibility, but deep down you'd rather just pay the money and save yourself the headaches. We'll cope with kids some more in Chapter Six.

This chapter is just about figuring out one thing: Where is the guilt coming from?

Not a simple task. I know there are a couple of jokes in this book, but the fact is it's really serious. Guilt is a serious thing. Especially if you're Catholic. What? Forget it! You're not just dumping your wife. You're dumping your wife, your mother, your entire psyche, your background, your socialization from birth. Hellfire awaits you. Confess now, and you might be forgiven. Screw around behind her back, and your pious wife will pray for you. But for godssakes, don't mention divorce. Divorce is for heathens. They're going to hell anyway, but *you* have a chance! You're supposed to stick it out, don't you know that? Say a couple of Hail Mary's, make a donation, have a few beers, and go home.

Sounds great, right? Well, if you're not an ex-Catholic yet, you will be soon. You might as well sprout fangs and claws and wear a cape and carry a dagger around with you, because any day now you'll be turning into Satan.

Or, Christ, maybe you're a Jew. You were fed guilt at every meal along with the corned beef on rye with mustard. What did I ever do to you to deserve this? Tell me, 'cause I want to know. What did I do? Who do you think you are, Mister Country Club, Mister Stocks 'n Bonds? This woman (points to her chest with her thumb) bore your children! You think you're better than me? Better than everybody else who stays married for better or worse and suffers through it like you're supposed to? You better think twice, buster. My brother-in-law is a lawyer, and my daddy, and my uncle, and my best friend's sister, and on and on and on …

What if you're a WASP? Chances are, you're heaving a big sigh of relief right now. None of that is *your* bag. It's alien to you, all of it. In fact, you sort of feel like an alien. You wouldn't know what to feel about guilt or any of that stuff because, to tell the truth, you feel nothing but pure confusion. Okay, but don't tell anybody! Your guilt will surface soon enough, and when it does, you can read this chapter all over again.

Where is the guilt coming from? There's always a different answer for everyone, but the answers all eventually come down to the same thing. As a matter of fact, whether it's religious or social or just plain old fashioned guilt, it comes from ideology. Your religion may have a very powerful ideology, like the Catholic Church that tells you what to do every second of your life. Or it may have a social component, like the Jewish variety that comes in a hundred different flavors but always gives you the same stomach-ache every time. Or it may just be the world we live in. Single-parent families are bad. They are not what the doctor ordered, and they are responsible for most of the problems in this country. So that's a heavy rap to lay on a guy, right?

It's ideology. They can call it Family Values, but it's not left or right. It's popular politics. If this were Mao's Cultural Revolution, you'd be told to give everything to the commune. Ideologies change from time to time, but they always amount to the same thing: Making people live and act the way they're supposed to according to the social and political trends of the time. That's great if you've got a good wife.

You can just sail along with the good-guy spirit like a real hero. But a bad wife forces you to buck the system.

Hey, no one is saying that the nuclear family itself is just a trend. It's been around a long time. And you might like being married and have nothing against family values at all. If only you were married to someone else! That's the problem. You accidentally married the wrong person. Many people make that mistake. You can fix it.

First, fix your head. Work hard. Where is the guilt coming from? Analyze it. Take it apart. Study it. Break it down. It will take a while, but if you really want to, you can get a handle on your guilt. And if you do it systematically and intelligently, you will be better prepared to cope with the guilt when it rises up like bile in your throat or when it is aimed at your face by your wife like a loaded shotgun.

Chapter Four

With Or Without A Girlfriend

Girlfriends are always a very tricky subject. In this chapter, we'll talk about dumping your wife whether you have a girlfriend or you don't.

Guy With Girlfriend has a woman – truly in love and truly devoted – whom he loves and wants to marry and most important, really trusts. Guy Without Girlfriend has a few women in his life or a girlfriend who is not really serious about him, which amounts to not having a real girlfriend. This is important because Guy With Girlfriend will do things and make certain moves that Guy Without Girlfriend should not. So "girlfriend," here, is defined as the one-and-only, who'll be with you all the way. Other women who are not strictly defined as girlfriends can help with emotional solace and distraction and even peace of mind, but they should not be brought into the financial fold.

Do you have a girlfriend? If so, does she meet the strict criteria above? If not, your act follows the path of Guy Without Girlfriend. When it comes to money, you better be pretty sure that things are going to work out between the two of you. If you're not absolutely certain that you'll be together forever, then keep your money matters to yourself. (If you're asking yourself how someone can be "absolutely certain" right now, then you're Guy Without Girlfriend, okay?)

Guy With Girlfriend means romantic lyrics:

> *True blue,*
> *What do I do?*
> *I'll go through hell*
> *To be with you.*

If this rings a bell in your head, if your girlfriend is the absolute love of your life, congratulations. You're in a complicated, exciting, screwed-up mess. You're alive!

You might also be in big trouble. You have to make her calm down and be patient. She wants you now, but you have to take your time. Keep her a secret. Remember, your wife is incredibly suspicious, and you want to keep wifey in the dark as long as possible. Tell your girlfriend to hold her horses.

In the meantime, begin to bring small things to her house or apartment. What won't your wife notice? A little trophy or your trumpet? Some of your at-home files? Your good suit? Some books? Whatever you can sneak out at this point should be gradually shifted to your girlfriend's abode. Records, tapes, videos – look for things that might not be missed. If it's summer, take your boots, gloves, skis, whatever. If it's winter, take your swimming suit, a few summer clothes; you get the picture.

Whatever you do, don't get caught! Watch out for the kids. Watch out for the wife. It might be hard to find a time when no one's home. This is tricky, and it's a better idea to stick things in your briefcase or a backpack very noncha-lantly and carry them out right in front of everybody.

Back to the girlfriend. Don't get messy about your tim-ing and forget your normal schedule for doing things. Don't miss dinner and stay late at work and all of that. Not now. Now is the time to be good. And whatever you do, don't write any checks to your girlfriend, admit you're seeing her, move your mutual fund into her account, or anything else that will later be thrown up into your face by a pack of raven-ing lawyers.

Right now you want to get some stuff over there. Use your girlfriend's phone to make the calls you need to make. Get important papers out of your office and into her place. Do you have the deed to your house? Your rental lease? Your contracts for your insurance policies? Plan to give the lawyers photocopies; you keep the originals. Look around for coins, stamp collections, stock certificates.

Anything that belongs to you and your wife is as much yours as hers. Better in your hot little hands than in hers. The judge might give her the house, but she's going to need that deed, right? Possession gives you leverage.

And speaking of houses, here's a big question: Should you move? If you have a girlfriend, you'll probably be mov-ing in with her when you walk out. Maybe you should both move somewhere else, far away. Check the tables in the back of this book. Is your state a simple one with incompatibil-ity as grounds? You'll get a divorce sooner if it is. Then you can marry your girlfriend and go on fighting for your mon-ey and your kids for years to come. Or you can get out now. Get your money, get your girlfriend if you have one, and get the hell out of there. Check the tables again. Oh, no, you say. My state is a backwater dungeon. Holy cow! It's a holding pen for wayward husbands. Get serious about getting out before the lawyers lock you up.

Is your girlfriend the adventurous type who would live in a grass hut in Cambodia just to be with you? Or is she totally tied down: Job, family, massive roots dug deep into the ground? And what about you? Your business, your kids, your parents, your favorite football team? It's hard to pick up and leave your life behind. But maybe your life sucks, and that's exactly what you want to do – leave it behind. Each guy has his own gig. All I'm saying is, if you want to leave, decide now so that you have time to plan before your wife gets out her big guns.

Whether you decide to stay or go in the long run, you're here now. Your girlfriend is here too. You've got to know what you're going to do the night your wife slams the door behind you.

Consider some practical details. What about your mail? Are you going to forward it to her place? What about your phone? Are you going to give out her number as your own? Think about these questions, while I talk to Guy Without Girlfriend.

Okay, man. The women are out there, but for now you're on your own. You have an easier time with respect to moving because you don't have to bring someone else with you. On the other hand, kids can make moving hard. Or your work might make you feel stuck, more or less. But if you're in a bad-news state, you should give some serious thought to moving, or at least to having a second residence in another state.

In the meantime, you need a place to go when you walk out on your wife. Don't pick an apartment in a neighborhood where everyone knows you. Go to the other side of town, for chrisssakes. You want a place you can stand, too – not a miserable hole in the wall that will remind you everyday of all you gave up just to be alone. In other words, don't rent a room in some sleazy hotel to save money. This doesn't really save money (they're not that cheap anymore) and it's bad for your head. Get something decent. After all, you may be bringing some as yet unknown women there. Don't go nuts, though, and create a bachelor pad with wall units and lava lamps. This is your reality. Give it a look that says who you are – and if you're not really sure, read some magazines to find out. Nothing too extravagant, or you'll hear about it for certain. But don't deprive yourself, either.

One day soon, or one night, you're going to be walking out for good. Why not have a place ready so that when that door slams behind you, you have a decent place to go? Sign a short lease. You don't know what's going to happen. Open a checking account for your rent checks and other checks that are nobody's business. And, hey, don't throw a party at your new pad. Be discreet.

Once you have your place, do what Guy With Girlfriend is doing. Move some stuff over, a little at a time. Get your important papers out. Check your office for anything you might want to keep. But be sure to leave your wife's picture on your desk. She checks it every time she walks in, you know. And watch out for the secretary, if you have one. You're probably the most intriguing thing in her life. Don't get her worked up either. Be smooth. Be steady. Be the way you've always been.

Let's get back to Guy With Girlfriend. Remember, she has to hold her horses. That's hard for her. It's especially hard if she's in the closet. Poor thing. Some girlfriends will already be out in the open. Either the wife knows about her or you decided not to hide your love (big mistake), and everyone already knows you're a couple. If that's the case, it's done. You might as well have your mail sent there, use her phone, move in with her, and the whole bit. Unfortunately, you'll pay dearly for this convenience. But you'll also be able to live together without sneaking around.

If your sweetie is still a secret, you might be thinking, Why hold out any longer? Once I leave my wife, why not let the cat out of the bag? Here's why: Having a girlfriend is a *great big* disadvantage for you and a huge advantage for your wife in a divorce. She'll already have everyone's sympathy vote, but if you have a young and beautiful girlfriend, they'll want to skin you alive and they will. The judge, the lawyers (including your own) will have no sympathy for you, will not listen to a word you say, will make you pay twice as much of everything, and will serve the girlfriend with papers too. A man who dumps his wife for a younger woman makes people's blood boil. You're in love, you're happy, you're getting great sex every day – people hate that! Listen up. It's a fact of life in our joke-a-minute justice system: If you have a girlfriend, you will pay more. Thousands more.

So if it's not too late, keep her hidden. Buy her beautiful things, tell her what you're up to, and let her read this book. Watch out for sleazy investigators with zoom lenses. Yes, it happens a lot on TV. But don't think it won't happen to you if you're not careful.

Give your girlfriend the benefit of the doubt. Tell her about your plans. Ask her to be patient. Of course, she loves you. And she probably doesn't want your wife to confront her with a kitchen knife or boil her pet rabbit anyway. She'll see the sense in holding out if she knows you're serious about her, and you are. Be sure to describe the financial benefits for both of you because, take my word for it, the whole divorce will cost thousands of dollars more if they know about your girlfriend.

If you can hold out and if your girlfriend can wait it out, you'll be each other's reward after a long, hot battle. There will be times when she will be your only comfort. She's the only one who will know what you're going through. She's going to start thinking that *she* was married to that woman and that *she* lived with those kids. But she's the one who gets the big reward in the end: You. And you get her. And when it's all over, if it ever is, you will have been through a lot more than plain old couples ever go through. That kind of thing brings you closer. Everyone will want you to break up under the strain of the divorce, but you'll stay together … for love. It's worth waiting for. It's beautiful, ain't it? Painful, but beautiful.

Girlfriend or not, the temptation, when you decide to dump your wife, is to make a clean, fast break. *This is a fantasy.* Once you get married, there is no such thing as a clean, fast break unless you have millions of dollars hidden in a foreign country, and you're planning to fake your own death. (Hmmm. Not a bad idea! We'll get to that in the next chapter.) The real story is a grind. The slow, clop-clop sound of jackasses working in law offices and courtrooms, chomping away on people's lives.

Be systematic. Plan your moves. If you have a girlfriend, help her hang in there. If not, you can handle it on your own. Stay alert. Get your place ready. And get yourself some great sex to keep you going.

Chapter Five

Hide Your Money!*

Take this short quiz:

1. What is the most important thing in a divorce? Answer: **Your money**.

2. What drives the divorce industry? Makes lawyers rich? Makes angry wives go shopping?
Answer: **Your money**.

3. What's the one thing that your wife, the lawyers, the judge, and maybe even your kids will keep on demanding until you're a homeless welfare recipient sitting on the street with a tin cup and a sad dog?
Answer: **Your money**!

---

*This book is FOR ENTERTAINMENT PURPOSES ONLY and should not be construed in any way to provide legal advice. Indeed, some of the actions referenced in this book may be ILLEGAL in your jurisdiction. UNDER NO CIRCUMSTANCES SHOULD YOU UNDERTAKE ANY ACTIVITIES IN RELIANCE ON THIS BOOK. SEEK PROFESSIONAL ADVICE BEFORE PROCEEDING. **As a first step, you may wish to arrange a confidential consultation with a qualified and reputable asset protection specialist at www.divorceassetprotection.com, who can assist you in dealing honestly and wisely with the IRS and other government authorities.**

Sorry to be so blunt, but your feelings are meaningless, your marriage is meaningless, your best intentions are meaningless. Only one thing has meaning in a divorce, and that's your money.

"I'll pay!" "I'll pay!" you cry. And they'll be glad to hear it. The problem with your willingness is that it will never go far enough. You will never be able to pay enough. If you had a wife who said, "Okay, Joe, that's fair, that's enough for me" – you wouldn't need this book, would you? Nope. But if you know in your guts that you need every bit of advice you can get, then listen up. Read this chapter carefully. Read it twice. Then read it again.

Maybe you've got nothing to hide. If you're basically broke or you only make a small amount of money and you have no savings, you don't have much to worry about. What can they take? They'll take your paychecks until maybe you quit. Or you keep working and let the money go to your wife. It's pretty simple. There's that one source of income. First, they'll tell you to hand over most of it. If you don't, they'll simply help themselves. Eventually, your wife and her lawyer will take whatever they know you have, a car or a truck, for example. And if it's not much more, that's the end of the story. If you leave town, they'll make a few cursory efforts to find out if you're earning anything, and if not, they'll leave you alone and just talk about what a rat you are. The point is, if they know you're not worth much money, you're pretty safe. What's the worst thing they can do? Throw you in jail? Your wife would enjoy that, but even then she won't get any money out of you if you don't have it.

The bad thing for a guy in your shoes is that they won't let you pay for the kids directly. You can never make sure that the money they take from you has any benefit for your kids. Often it doesn't. The courts should be able to set up an escrow fund for the kids and oversee the spending of it. They could do this. They do it for wives all the time. But they refuse to do it. They insist on giving all child support to the wives no matter what the women do with the money. This is part of the bias against men in the divorce courts. There's nothing you can do about it except, maybe, try to hide some money away to give your kids when they're a little older … if they'll still speak to you, that is.

The point is, your wife will get paid until there's nothing left to pay. If she thinks you're broke, she'll probably try to find some other guy to pay her bills, and then you'll be off the hook. Unless you ever do make money.

Which brings us to the next problem: Men who have money.

Have you worked hard all your life? Have you struggled to put something away for your future? Have you had an enormously successful medical practice or business deal that really put you over the top? Great income, nice vacations, terrific houses and cars? How about those mutual funds, stock options, life insurance policies? What about your Keogh? Your IRA? Will they take your long-term bond portfolio? They will! They'll take it all, eventually.

"But I live in California. They can only take half." Ho, Ho, Ho, Santa! They'll start with half, but then they'll say, "Gee, maybe half is not half. Let's see all of your statements from all of your brokers all over again. It's been six months and maybe we missed a few dividends here, an interest payment there. And your wife's lawyer has to be paid, and yours too, don't forget. Let's just have ourselves another look at all of your cancelled checks for the past five years *again*. And what's this fancy restaurant bill? You're going out to restaurants while your poor wife is starving? Maybe we'll need to reevaluate your stock plan. It will only take two years. It will only cost you twenty thousand ..."

STOP! Read this: *You can and will run out of money unless you hide some right now.*

"But won't they accuse me of hiding my assets?"

Of course! If you stick a gold pen in a drawer, you'll be accused of hiding assets. It's standard procedure these days. Every wife's lawyer in America gets down on all fours in front of the judge and howls like a wolf at the full moon.

"He's hiding the marital assets, *Owwwoooowwooo!*"

And the judge (a lawyer with a robe on, remember) looks down from Mount Olympus and cries, "Freeze them! Seize them! Off with his head!"

Wouldn't it be nice, at this moment of supreme civic unrest, if you had a few dollars tucked away? If you had already moved some of your money into friendly foreign hands?

When they ask you where you hid your money, you can gaze up at that goose face on the bench and say, "Your Honor, I would never do a thing like that."

Are you with me? Okay. The best way to hide your money is in a tax haven overseas. Many businessmen already know about these things, but this chapter is for the guys who don't. Maybe you're an artist or a surgeon or a freelance zoologist and you don't know beans about business. Maybe you've played it kind of close to the vest, Mister All-American, and you always felt that the major American brokers and banks were fine for you. And they were. But they're not now.

First, report your income. All of it. You don't want to play into your wife's hands by enlisting the IRS. We'll talk more about the IRS later. So report it all. Then get it the hell out of here.

The tricky part is the damn paper trail that money leaves behind these days. The foreign banks won't call up your wife and say, "Hey, guess what?" But they will hand over your account if they get a court order. That means if you screw up and she finds out what you're doing, bye-bye money. So we're going to make it almost impossible for that to happen.

Most private investigators will run your social security number through databases in your state. If they run it through other states, their fee goes up and up. A foreign run will cost your wife about ten grand. The beauty is that most foreign banks don't use your social security number. So they can't track you all over Asia by punching your number into a computer. But do your research and inquire with the bank since there's always the chance that some shifting anti-terrorism laws may require you to tweak your strategy. Don't worry though – your foreign banker knows the game and can help you navigate the Executive Orders so you can jump through the right legal loopholes. You should also do some of your own reading and consulting. Again, you can get a head start at www.divorceassetprotection.com.

Your job is to keep your account secret. Don't write it down. Don't carry around your foreign banker's business card in your wallet. People have been caught that way. *And don't tell anyone, especially not your friends.*

"Gee, Susan, I really feel bad for you. Joe is my best friend, it's true. But he's hiding money from you, and I think you should know about it. So here's all the information he gave me in confidence. Now, how about dinner tonight?"

Don't tell *anyone* about your accounts!

As for the paper trail, that's more difficult. It's tricky. You can't just write a check to your account in the Caymans because it will come back to your bank with a stamp on it. When your wife's lawyer subpoenas your bank records, your cancelled check to the not-so-secret account will be found. A court order will follow.

The paper trail. Any check, wire transfer, letter of credit, or even a traveller's check can be easily traced.

"No way am I going to start carrying around bags of cash like a mobster or a dope dealer," you say.

Right, that won't do. And, remember, *you are not a crook.* Sometimes, during a divorce, after sufficient harassment, that's hard for you yourself to believe.

First, when you liquidate your accounts, get the money broken up into two or three checks, if at all possible. Be discreet. Don't explain anything to anyone you deal with, and if you feel uncomfortable asking, then don't ask. Don't have the checks sent out to your home or office and don't tell the bankers your private mailbox address. Go there and pick up the checks yourself. Then get a tax ID number from the IRS for a sole proprietor. You can say you're starting a lifesaver training business (and in a sense it will be true). When you're a sole proprietor, you can pick any business you want and call it whatever you want. Now you have a tax ID number to use instead of your social security number. Again, shift your strategy as necessary to fly under the radar.

Okay, start opening accounts. Get bank accounts. Go to stock brokers. Go to discount brokerage firms. Get check-writing accounts at credit unions. Go to other states, far away if possible, and open up some small accounts. Use your private mailbox as your address. If you can, use a retail mailbox service with a street address instead of the U.S. Postal Service. The service will be better, and they're more discreet. Vary your name. Use initials, use your middle name. Use your business name. You can put any name you want on an account.

Now begin to move your money. Shove it around and around and around. Make withdrawals. Write checks to yourself. You won't need to resort to cash transactions because your accounts will be so mixed-up, complicated, and confusing that it would take too much money for your wife to track them all down. And she'd need a few leads. And she won't have any!

Eventually. you'll be able to get large amounts into a few obscure accounts and write checks on them to foreign banks. After all, you won't have the FBI tracking you down. You're not doing anything illegal. It's your money, for godssakes. You can spend all your time talking to boring bank clerks if you feel like it. It's your right as an American. Unfortunately, it does take time, a lot of time. So what? In the end it's worth it!

But if your wife finds even one account, just one, you're in trouble. That's why you have to be careful with the tax ID number and careful with the address. If you have a girlfriend, you can use her address. But it's better to have your own secret address because your wife might be spying on your girlfriend, too.

Remember, keep the money moving and churning. Don't get lazy. Use S&L's, use big banks, little banks. Go to foreign exchanges and get some colorful currencies. Then buy back a cashier's check for US dollars – pesos for greenbacks. It's legal. Get your bucks moving. Trade, transfer, turn around. Don't relax!

Once you've got everything in a tremendous tangled mess, you're ahead of the game. That's right, man. You're fouling up the paper trail. Then you can concentrate on other things, like where to put your funds overseas. These days the one trendy place to go is the Cayman Islands. But beware – all dumped wives look there first. They think you're going down there with some woman to scuba dive and hide money, and they're right. That's what most guys do. So don't do it. Do something else.

The Bahamas will give you the same banking deal, but you have to watch out for drug crimes there. You don't want to be one of those poor schnooks sitting in a Bahamian prison because someone robbed you and put a joint in your pocket. On the other hand, if you're hip to the crime scene or at least careful about where you go and what you do abroad and you don't want to travel far, the Bahamas may be a good bet. They have banks there that don't do business in the U.S. That's what you want. Don't go to some friendly, hometown-sounding bank like the Bank of Anywhere USA and figure that it's okay because it's located overseas. Nope, it's not okay. It could end up being your worst nightmare. You need banks that *do not do business in the U.S.*

Another good thing about the Bahamas is that you can pretend you lost all your money gambling there, if your wife and the lawyers want to know.

"Hey, where's this Merrill Lynch account that was closed on such-and-such a date?" her lawyer might ask.

"Oh, *that* account," you say with a heavy sigh.

"Well, gee, I got so depressed I flew to Paradise Island and lost it all on blackjack."

They won't believe it, of course, but bring back a few chips and they can't disprove it.

So here you are in Nassau. Hmmmmm. Tacky. Piña Coladas. Run-down bars and too much afternoon rain. You go downtown and look for a bank. You'll see brass plates with names you never heard of. Go into one of these places. Tell the girl you want to talk to a banker about making a deposit. Wear a suit and tie. Look good. When the guy comes out, tell him you're in a bad divorce and he'll listen to your story. Ask him if his bank has branches in the U.S. If he says yes, forget it. Ask him if he will recommend a bank that doesn't. Chances are he will be from Switzerland or the Netherlands or some other European country.

When you find a place to rest some of your weary money, you'll show your passport, pick a code name, and arrange to have your mail held. You'll notice that these bankers are not like American bankers. They're actual humans! They look at you and talk to you and give you personal service. The same will be true if you go to Switzerland or Luxembourg or any other of the top foreign banking centers. If you've only dealt with American bankers, you'll be shocked by the difference. What? An educated person with a real vocabulary? A thinking individual? It's strange and exciting.

There are more centers for banking secrecy around the world these days than ever before. It seems like everyone is trying to get into the act. Since there is no privacy, let alone secrecy, in American banking, there's a big demand for it overseas. You can choose the Channel Islands, Malaysia, or even the Cook Islands near Australia. And there's even a little island out in the Pacific called Vanuatu, if you go for really exotic places.

Much depends on how much money you have to hide and how much risk you like to take. You don't want your money to end up in some obscure country that's going to erupt into revolution one day soon. And you don't want to choose the bank that all the drug lords are flocking to either. You'll need to do some research if you want to go off the beaten track.

If you want to be safe, go to Switzerland or Luxembourg or Liechtenstein. They specialize in wealthy individuals, and they'll help you out even if you're not a millionaire. Certain banks won't take you if you have less than a hundred thousand dollars for a starter, but others will. Remember – make sure they don't do business in the U.S. A restraining order on a branch in your home state can wreak havoc on your accounts abroad.

Thanks to the drug lords and terrorists, you can't keep your identity secret from the foreign bankers anymore. You used to be able to go to a lawyer overseas and get him to open a numbered account for you so that even the banks didn't see your face. But the Islamo-fascists and the Columbian cartels wrecked that for the rest of us, and now you have to go to the bank yourself and tell them who you are. The good news is they don't care.

You're not a crook, so they're not worried about you or your money. And I'll say this again, unless you get sloppy, your wife will never know about your account. In other words, she can't just get on the phone and call every bank in Europe and ask them if they know you. She won't get a straight answer. She won't ever know about your foreign accounts unless you screw up and tell her or tell someone else who tells her but it won't be your foreign bankers. *They* are discreet.

Oh, by the way, you might have heard that it's not a crime to avoid the IRS in Switzerland. Lots of people think this is a dandy place to earn interest and dividends tax free – and it is. The problem begins when you bring the money back to America to spend it. BAM! Tax City. So don't tuck away too much money if you're going to need it in the near future. What you stow away should be excess cash for your kids' college fund or your retirement or fake death – if you have enough dough and guts to pull *that* off.

Seriously, there are ways, as many movie stars and other rich people have discovered, of bringing money back here without giving a huge chunk of it to the government. I'm talking about complicated loans with cute names and stuff like that. But if you're rich enough to get into those shenanigans, you don't need me to tell you how to do it.

So back to your secret bucks in the faraway bank. It's neat to be like 007. You buy your plane ticket with cash. You wear dark glasses. You'll see. It's lots of fun, and it will help you feel better while your wife and her lawyers are sucking your income through a straw. If they find out you hid some money, they'll cry foul. They'll say you did it to "intention-ally waste the marital assets before distribution." And, of course, you did. The point is, they won't find out. When they ask where certain monies went, you plead insanity or take the fifth or sit in prison for a day or two if necessary. Bring something to read. Don't worry; they can't keep you there for long because it's a civil case.

Remember, it's just a short hop from spilling the beans to losing all your beans. You won't tell. You better not. After all, you want to have something left for your kids when you die. And you need to live on something before you die. You won't tell. You won't. Sometimes it's hard to imagine the devastation of divorce before it takes place. You might underestimate your wife's fury or her desire for revenge. You might underestimate the ruthlessness of the lawyers and judges.

You might think this whole book is a little extreme. Well, it is.

Some people get divorced, case closed, it's over, and they go on with their lives. But some don't. Some women nev-er get over being dumped, and they never stop looking for their revenge. You know. If you have one of those women at home right now, sure, you *know*.

A little extreme? You bet. Just remember this: You are not a criminal. Even if they try to throw you in jail for con-tempt, yours is a civil case, a divorce. Your wife might try to turn you into a criminal by accusing you of molesting your kids or stealing or something. ***But you are not a crim-inal.*** You are just being treated like one. Don't let them win! Don't rush into the court room and shoot your wife and spend your life in prison. She's not worth it. Fight the good fight, instead. Be smart. Be sneaky. And leave her bitterness behind.

Chapter Six

What About Your Kids?

There's no easy answer to this question. It is by far the hardest part of dumping your wife. You might have one kid or you might have five. They could be in high school or in preschool. Everyone's situation is different. You might be madly in love with your kids or indifferent to them or worried about them or sick of them. It's hard to address such a wide spectrum and impossible for anyone but you to really understand your feelings about your own kids. But the hardest part of all is when you contemplate what your leaving will do to your relationship with them.

One steady principle applies to most guys who are dying to get out of a marriage: You are not happy. It's that simple. If you were happy, you wouldn't be dumping your wife. You're just not happy. Your wife, even if she knows things aren't great between you, would probably be perfectly happy if you stayed put. So would your kids. The status quo would make everyone happy but you. This is *your* happiness we're talking about, for once.

So what's going to happen? Consider your wife. Is she basically a decent person? Will she be able to control herself enough to give a couple of passing thoughts to the psychic welfare of your children? If so, you're in luck. You can always say, "Let's think of the kids first. Let's try to do what's best for them. Let's be civil."

Some wives are like this. A few. Their kids, their new husbands, and their ex-husbands are a lucky bunch. Hooray for them. But what about the silent majority of men who are married to Gila monsters in drag? What about you?

Get out the knives! Get out the hypodermics! Your new life begins with lacerations of guilt and massive injections of poison. What's the name of her game? It's called GET REVENGE. A whole new realm of pain is opening up to you. Your children's pain. It hurts a lot more than your own. You wish she'd cut into you with her searing remarks and just leave the kids out of it. But, no. She knows how to operate, and she knows her victim very, very well.

That voice. It's always there.

Your father hates you! He abandoned you! He's destroying our family, and he doesn't care about you anymore. He doesn't love you. He never loved you. All he cares about is himself. Look at the way he's living! What about us? We have nothing. He has everything. He's ruined your life. He's evil. He should be in prison. Your father is the biggest asshole ever to walk on this earth, and if you ever see him again, I'll never forgive you!

Does reading this make you a little nervous?

Do you sort of cringe when you think of your innocent little kids eating this load of crap for dinner every night?

It's true that divorce is a traumatic and difficult experience for kids to endure. They love you, and they want you around, providing stability and togetherness as usual. You see their faces, and you know they're thinking *Don't leave us!* They would prefer your presence even if you and your wife fight every day. They don't want you to leave. They don't want divorce.

How can they know what it will be like? Maybe she won't be as bad with them if you're not around to witness her hysterics. Maybe your absence will create a vacuum, a sort of calm, a steady stream of complaints rather than her screeching, angry fear of divorce that your kids have been enduring all this time.

Or it could come as a complete shock to your kids. Maybe they mistook your absence or a coldness between you and wife for a regular household. How are they supposed to know? They've never lived in other families. They simply don't know.

Many kids cope with divorce. Kids have been coping with it for decades. They function. They see their dads. They stick it out and make it all right. Those are usually the kids with the decent mothers. The ones who are capable of acknowledging the fact that the kids still love their dad, the man who is leaving her. This kind of woman cares about that relationship because she knows it can still be beneficial for the kids, even if it is painful for her. Oh, man. We're back talking about that lucky bunch again. Wishful thinking is easy when it comes to kids.

Unfortunately, most of the guys reading this book are not members of the lucky bunch. Whatever your wife does, whatever your situation is, you can't blame yourself if your wife is bent on sacrificing your kids to the great god of revenge. That's right. They will be her most potent and dangerous weapon.

And you can't save them from her. Even if you did bite the bullet and stay married to her until the kids grow up, they'll be scarred by your misery and her suspicions. They'll miss out on one of life's finest lessons: Love exists. Two people can live together, loving each other daily and deeply. Kids who witness the other kind of family life, whether it's coldness or fighting or living a lie, grow up without that truth in their own childhoods.

It takes a lot of guts to live an authentic life, especially if you've got a comfortable sham all set up, especially if taking the rough road is going to cause your kids some pain. It's up to you. You've only got one life, man. Kids count. They depend on you. They grow up and leave you. They *are* you in a way, by extension. What kind of authentic life do you have to offer them?

The most important thing to remember from this chapter is *your kids will survive. Your relationship with them might not survive. But your kids will survive.*

So what's my wife going to do? Let's look at a few of the wife-types and see if we can predict this.

Wife One will probably react the best. She's the passive, stand-by-your-man type with her head in the sand. She doesn't want pain or trouble; in fact, she doesn't even know how to handle it. She'll probably cry a lot, shoulders to the wind, and resolve to take care of the children. She'll martyr herself by working overtime (even if you're paying more than enough). She'll slave away at the housework like never before. She'll weep. She'll work. Weep and work. Deep down, she still loves you and believes that you will always be her husband.

For you, Wife One is a drag. She's so heavy on the guilt that you begin to lose it. How guilty can one guy feel? What the hell. Here. Take a Kleenex. You do your best with Wife One. She's not a bad person. She means well. And for your kids, she's a decent deal. They may even be better off staying with her instead of coming with you. She might agree later on to joint custody, hoping to see you frequently. She won't badmouth you that much to the kids. She cares about them. But she doesn't want to let go of you. So between the guilt and giving in to her demands, you'll be dancing a fine line with Wife One. Still, it's worth it to know that your kids are not being tortured. You're practically lucky if you're married to a Wife One.

Not you, if you've got a Wife Two. Remember her? The crafty French-peasant type who has been anticipating your departure all along? Watch out! This one is real trouble. Here's the woman who will fight to the death for revenge at the expense of her own children. Poison is her middle name. You may realize, for the first time, that your kids are already allied with her, even though you haven't said yet you're leaving. She's been planning for this, and she wants them firmly on her side. Come to think of it, hasn't she always sided with the kids against you in the past? Eureka! This woman will be happy to parade her children through the courts, proclaiming your lechery and beastly behavior in front of anyone who will listen. Wife Two pulls out the big sex-abuse guns later on in the custody case. She's just getting revved up now.

You might find yourself talking to yourself. How can she do this to her own kids? How can she talk about this sex stuff? When did she get such a foul mouth? Doesn't she care how they feel? About their confusion? Why is she making it worse for them instead of trying to make it easier? Doesn't she love them?

Get it now. Those kids were born but they might as well have been purchased before the arms reduction treaty. They were conceived as weapons to hold on to you and, if necessary, to destroy you. Believe it. Wife Two is too insecure to love anyone but herself. Her proclamations are empty screams of contempt. She knows you never loved her. She's known it all along. And now she's going to use her own kids to pay you back.

You probably won't even want to attempt a custody battle with Wife Two. And if you try it, you'll probably lose. Lawyers rarely understand human nature, and they surely don't have a clue when it comes to the sub-human woman. If you ask them, of course, they'll say fight, fight, fight. That's just your money going into their pockets. But they don't have any idea about what you're up against when you've got a Wife Two on your hands. Custody? Sure, they'll take you through the paces, and then several thousand dollars later they'll do the famous lawyer-shrug in court. Shrug. Shrug. Sorry, sucker.

We'll come back to custody in a little while. First, let's take a look at Wife Three. She's a bit of a puzzle, isn't she? Certainly, she's not as wild or miserable as Wife Two. But she's not as mild and meek as Wife One either. She's more businesslike, more calculating. Likely as not, she'll want full custody, but she'll have to fight for it. Your marriage to her might have been pretty decent at one time, and you did share and share alike: Things, money, kids. Those kids will be torn. They like you both. But Wife Three will be convinced that she'll be better at raising them because she's better at everything. She knows everything. She's full of ideology, and she always uses the word "parent" as a verb. So she'll fight hard. Beware. You'll need to psyche her out and win your kids over before you drop the bomb.

What to do? For all you guys who can work it out one-on-one reasonably and in the best interest of the kids, good for you!

For the other ninety percent of mankind, whose children will be held hostage by scorned rabid animals, get ready. Always anticipate the worst. Even Wives One and Three can lay a heavy load on your kids, especially your first year out of the house. It hurts them, and it sure hurts you. So get ready for the truly bad part of dumping your wife.

First of all, do you really want your kids to live with you? Can you handle the school lunches, the sickness, the little friends, the constant video games? Can you handle the demands on your time? Do you have room in your new place? If you have a girlfriend, does she want them? Do they want her? If your kids move in with you, you'll need a housekeeper, a nanny, or a new wife right away. Or maybe all three! You'll need real meals for dinner, two televisions, even a toaster. It's a big job. All of those complaining single mothers out there really do have tough lives. But they do have custody of their kids. (Don't you think they should have to give up custody if they complain about it too much? There should be a legal limit to the amount of bitching and moaning we have to hear when a woman wins custody. That's what

I think. Harumph.) If you want to keep your kids, it will be a big hassle, but it might be worth it too. Nevertheless, think hard in advance about the logistics.

So you want custody? Or at least joint custody? Can you make a case for an unfit mother? Start now. Try to take a picture of your wife smoking a joint or in a drunken stupor. Can you get her to dance with some other guy at a party? Take a picture! Call your friends late at night from a pay phone and ask them if she's there, or if they've seen her. Get some videos of the real woman, when she really looks like hell. Check the medical records for bills from shrinks. This is particularly good for Wife Three who has probably had years of therapy. Write down the names of all the tranquilizers she's ever used.

This approach is especially effective with Wife Three. She lets her guard down because she thinks she's invincible. She's always right. She knows everything. She doesn't have to worry about protecting herself. And, above all, she believes that everyone in the world must play by her rules. Even you.

Here is something else about Wife Three. It's an ideological conundrum: Weren't you expected to be a "co-parent?" Remember that term? Weren't you there with bells on when the baby came and happy to help out with diapers and late-night feedings and day-care visits and mushed-up carrots, the whole baby experience? Didn't you nurture your nuts off? Hey! They want you to work when you're not there and when you are there, but when they don't want you there you don't have any rights anymore. Hey! Being a thirty-something father should guarantee you automatic joint custody. Why should the woman get the kids when you were just as much of a mother as she was? How handy. Being a woman is very convenient when it's a simple excuse for a legal advantage. You did the drudge work too. Suddenly your nurturing is not as good as hers?

Let's go back to **Wife Two** now. She needs the most attention because a belligerent feminist is nothing compared to Our Lady of Lechery – Wife Two, who thinks that every single "single" woman should be caged. The wife who checks your underwear for lipstick. Good god. The older kids might be infused with her spirit by now and lost to you. Or maybe not. Are they able to think for themselves? And the little ones are breaking your heart. Now, what are you going to do if you have kids with this woman and you can't stand the idea of leaving them with her, of having them raised by a bitter burned cat? What the hell are you going to do?

Start by expecting the worst out of her and the most out of yourself. If you have a girlfriend, lean on her. If you don't, lean on yourself.

Here is the worst possible thing you can expect from Wife Two: The sex abuse accusation. Yes, she'll do it if the kids are young enough. It's disgusting all right, but it happens all the time.

Not only will it ruin your life, but it destroys the chances of little kids who go into court with sad but very true stories, hoping to be believed. False accusations give defense lawyers ammunition to use against defenseless little kids who have actually been sexually abused. Of course, the lawyers don't care. And neither does Wife Two. She doesn't give a damn about them. She cares about herself, and she's not about to pass up one of the most popular weapons in the custody arsenal.

It sucks. There's no denying it. You've heard about it, and you don't want it to happen to you. The worst part is that they get away with it time and time again. And it shouldn't happen at all. It's obvious to some of us when the sex abuse charge is made up. How can we tell? Because the fake accusations always come from the same source: Wife Two. Regular wives don't use their own children to *get revenge*. If a regular wife, even a woman such as a Wife One or a Wife Three or any woman who behaves like a responsible adult, makes an accusation of sexual abuse, people have to wonder. Hmmmm, what's going on here? But if it comes from the depths of hell, if it's soaked in the rancid spit of revenge, it's obvious! And – don't miss this – the charge is always sudden. What? You did that? After how many years? You want out and *all of a sudden* this abuse has been going on … for how long? Give us a break! Why didn't the good mother ever notice this *before* she got dumped? Someone should do a study of how often the sex abuse charge has come from wives whose husbands left them for younger women. That would be enlightening. But, man, don't hold your breath waiting for *that* study to come out.

If it happens to you – and I sure hope it doesn't – remember the old basic rule: The best defense is a good offense. Do you think, in your case, that it could happen? Then tell your lawyer to expect it. You might want to warn your pediatrician and your local police. Look out, folks, here's a mad one. Don't take her too seriously. She's going to say anything.

Most importantly, talk to your kids. She'll only do it to the little ones, the ones she can easily snow. So talk to them. Tell them that Mommy is very upset, and she might have some strange ideas. If Mommy starts talking about nasty things, call someone. Tell your child to call your sister or your mother or you. Give the child an out. Let your kid know that Mommy's not well.

This will give your child a boost of confidence when Mommy dearest begins to lather on the sex talk. It's sick, of course. But all you can do is try to warn your child and other people that you know it's coming. It would also be a good idea to bug the apartment, tap her phone, and spy on her. Try to get evidence of the corruption. Even if you can't use it in court, people will believe you if you have proof that she's lying.

Be realistic. Don't just walk around gritting your teeth, hoping it won't happen. Know your opponent. Be ready. She's going to try to get you where it hurts the most – your little kids. It happens all the time.

What's your offensive strategy?

We always hear about people who get caught up in this sick stuff. And what about those people who steal their own kids and run off to some place like Brazil? This is TV docu-drama material. Don't let it become your life story.

Be cool, be smart, be stronger than she is. Try to keep your feelings and your anger under control. Remember, you're leaving her. Expect a bad time, but don't go straight to the drastic measures. You want to keep some contact with your kids. In most cases it will be possible. You might even daydream about joint custody. Just take one day at a time.

When you do see the kids, what can you expect? If you've already left, they might be sent out to retrieve you with tears, threats, begging. Your wife might try to sabotage their homework to make it look like they're failing in school because of you. She might send them to you to bring back information for her. She'd like to know all about your apartment, your girlfriend, your lifestyle. Or she might – this is very common – not let you see your kids at all unless you pay more for the privilege. Selling children. How civilized. Selling them to their own father – despicable, right? But unbelievably common.

Expect the worst from your dumped wife.

Talk to your kids as often as you can before you leave and when you leave. Don't lie to them. Use the word *divorce*. Try to make them aware of their mother's problems and weaknesses. Reassure them. Tell them you'll always be there for them. They can always come to you. Warn them that Mommy is going to say a lot of bad things about you. Tell them why. Tell them they don't have to believe what she says and they don't have to answer her if they don't want to. Tell them they can always call you or come stay with you if they want to. Be explicit. Be thorough. Be straight with them.

Remember: Whatever you do about your kids, you're doing the best you can.

Once your case gets to court, no one is going to give a damn about your feelings for your kids. They will merely assume that you're a filthy piece of slime, a thief, a scumbag. Do I exaggerate? No. You never hear the politicians or the journalists or the preachers say, "That guy really loves his kids, and he'd like to be more involved in their lives."

No way. Now you're nothing but a money bag. The world doesn't want you. They want your money.

They don't care that this woman poisoned your children against you, tore their hearts out with vicious lies about you, and refuses to let you see them. So what? They want your money, and they'll keep you from your kids unless you pay whatever they want. Who is this "they?" Your wife, her lawyers, and her judge. Yes, they're selling children, but that's okay. They've got the trendy TV shows on their side, they're correct, and you are a man, which automatically makes you – guess what? – A DEADBEAT DAD! You're bad because you're the man. She's good because she's the woman. Therefore, it's okay for her to sell you your own children. Follow me?

I'm sure the Founding Fathers would be very proud of today's guardians of justice. Yeah, right. Don't expect anything from your own lawyer either. We'll get to the lawyers in Chapter Nine. And of course the judge will always be on your wife's side. So when your case gets to court, don't do any of these things:

1. Do not proclaim your love for your girlfriend.
2. Do not kidnap your kids.
3. Do not break down and cry.
4. Do not bring a gun to court.

You don't need a crystal ball to see that child support is going to be the bleating cry coming out of your sheep wife. Everything will hang on child support. Every whining trip your wife makes to her lawyer's office will be a complaint about how you've destroyed your children and how you're not paying her enough. Your own lawyer will upbraid you, lecture you, threaten you with prison. All in the name of child support.

You can calculate what you'll have to pay in advance. It's around 17% of your income per year for the first child and around 12% for each one after that. Off your gross. Be sure to add another 15% for miscellaneous expenses and another 5 to 10% for pure punishment. And it's not deductible. Supporting your kids will cost triple the amount you pay now.

But when you see your kids – if you get to – don't expect them to appreciate your efforts. They don't know about any money that you've been paying. All you hear from them is poor, poor, poor.

"But what about the $1500 a month I send for you?"

"Mommy says you don't pay."

Ain't that a bitch? But in fact you really do want to pay. You don't want to stiff your own kids, and you want them to know that you're taking care of them. So tell them! Argue your case in a simple way. You don't want them hearing only one side, *her* side. Don't take the high road. The high road leads to nowhere, when it comes to kids. It may be a waste to tell your side to a biased judge, but your kids do care. They love you, and they want to hear that you're not the monster she tells them you are. Talk to them. Don't leave them stranded on her side.

It's the best you can do, whatever you do. When it comes to kids, there are no jokes, no easy answers. As we said in Chapter One, if you leave when they're young, you're a vile, self-centered slimebag, but if you stay until they grow up, you're punished by the court for the length of the marriage.

Frankly, it's a no-win situation. Except for one thing. Kids grow. They grow and change. And you will always be their dad, no matter what she does to them and no matter how the world judges you. Some day your kids will be bigger, and they'll be interested in the truth. When that happens, if you've lost them for now, you'll have a chance again. A chance to talk to them and tell them how things really were in the divorce and in your heart. They're your kids, man. Forever. No matter what. Time is on your side.

Chapter Seven

Prepare To Unload

You're not ready yet. You've got to wait. Ever since you decided to dump your wife, she probably seems even more unbearable than ever. How did you stand it for so long? You just want to get away from her, be with your girlfriend, or be on your own. Suddenly, it seems as if you can't take another look at her without wanting to rush out the door. Something has clicked in you. In your mind you're almost free.

Unfortunately, you don't live in the Land of the Free. That's just a song. You live in the land of the trapped men. When was the last time a woman worried about losing her whole net worth because she wanted a divorce? Not lately. Let's see. Women don't want to be treated like objects or possessions, but they sure own their husbands, don't they?

Men are trapped. And there are thousands of self-righteous pinheads running around Washington trying to tighten the noose around your neck even more with laws that encourage you to get married and stay that way. They still cling to the notion that divorce is the work of the devil, and that only marriage can save us sinners (unless, of course, it's a gay couple who wants to take a spin on the marriage roulette wheel). We know from countless media reports that there are hordes of busybody activists who tout divorce as the root of all evil in modern society. Sure it is. And if the bozo doesn't realize it, we'll make him understand by forcing him to stay with her, by slapping him with court orders, garnishing his income, taking away his kids, and throwing him in jail, if we can.

So get with the program, guy. Your wife is divine and saintly, didn't you realize it?

The real message is this: Get out while there's still time. If the feminists, the ultra-conservatives, the pro-family freaks, and the goodness gurus get their way, you could be stuck forever.

Okay, okay. Let's make it happen. Yes, I want to do it. Dump my wife – Yes! Good for you! You're not being browbeaten into giving up your whole life for a woman you don't want or bending to the pressures of trendy ideology. You have a mind of your own, and you're putting it to work. But you still have preparations to make before you can leave.

This is not a legal text. (We'll talk about lawyers pretty soon. They get a whole chapter to themselves.) This is a survival manual. It's advice. Self-help – "self" being the operative word. Do you get it? You are on your own. And you're going to have to do some research.

Find out as much as you can about the divorce laws in your state and in any state you might be thinking of calling your own. You need to know more than what you can find in the back of this book, although it's a good start. So take a look at the tables right now. See your state? Check out some of the terminology. "Irreconcilable differences," "incompatibility," and "irretrievable breakdown" are all basically the same thing. Traditional grounds are the old-fashioned ones, such as she won't put out for you anymore or adultery or insanity or something. Check your state for grounds. What's the story?

Then you need to know more. There are all kinds of sneaky laws and tricky traps that differ from state to state. You need to find out as much as possible. Be informed! You can't do this by calling lawyers because, number one, they never give you a straight answer; and, number two, why pay several hundred dollars for information you can get your-self for free? Of course, you might want to hire someone who is not a lawyer – maybe a paralegal (they're cheap) or a freelance research assistant. You might want to check out a local research firm and see if they will do a fee-paid proj-ect without making you open a whole account. Any of these methods will yield more information than one or two expen-sive hours of lawyering.

I know what you're thinking. Don't use your secretary! Or anyone at your office, for that matter. Don't call around town or ask your friend's college-student son to do it. *Get someone you know from the other side of town.*

Or do it yourself, if you have time. Call the state capi-tol and ask for the Public Information Office. Ask them if they have any written materials about your state's divorce laws that they can send you for your "research project." Don't say, "I'm about to file for divorce and I want to know in advance where I stand." The lady on the phone will tell you to call your lawyer. Thanks a lot, lady. Just say you're a graduate student doing research. Push it, too. You're working on a big research problem about the effects of divorce on the middle class in your state. Blah, blah, blah. Whatever they've got, you want. Have it sent to your girlfriend's apartment or to your own new and private mailbox.

Then go to the university library nearest you and see what you can find there. This is real important for two reasons. One, you might be thinking of moving. Two, you have to know what you're doing before the lawyers sink their teeth into you. The divorce might drag on and on forever, but the court orders and the bills come right away. Before that happens, you want to find out as much as you can on your own.

You'll find out a lot of interesting things, too. In your research you'll read that there have been no-fault divorce laws on the books in all fifty states since the 1970s. Sounds good, right? Wrong. Whether on the books or not, those laws are worthless to you.

If your wife says, "Of course, Joe, let's get a divorce right away," great! That's called consent. Some people get it. Some people (remember the lucky bunch?) agree to break up. They don't need this book. They just smile and make a deal and walk away from each other. The no-fault laws are for them.

But if your wife says, "Up yours, buddy," you can just kiss the whole idea of no-fault goodbye. It's a crock. Sure, she can't stop the divorce itself – you'll get one, all right. But you can still spend ten years fighting over kids and money after that. She has a claim on you for as long as she feels like following you around. And if she doesn't make you fight, chances are her lawyer will.

You'll find another popular deception in your research: All women suffer in poverty after a divorce. Who made this one up? Yeah, if you call sitting around collecting your money while somebody else works "suffering." Sounds like intense pain to me. They really suffer, especially the ones who get the house, the kids, monthly maintenance, child support, your life insurance, your car, your dead mother's homemade candlesticks. That's real suffering.

Meanwhile, you're paying all of her rent/mortgage, expenses, health care, and trying to feed your own face once in a while. You never ate so many hotdogs in your life!

All right, some women do suffer. They live in the 'hood. They have four or five children, a drug habit, no education, and, frankly, a hopeless life to begin with. These women make great research subjects, and you'll be coming across a lot of them. But what does that have to do with you? Not much.

Your wife is about to win the lottery of her life. The great Entitlement Act of Feminism. You've heard it. We want to be respected and given responsibility at the office and promoted. But we also want to be protected, paid for, and given someone else's earnings on a silver platter when our poor little hearts get broken. What a great deal!

Your research is going to teach you a lot about the big gap between popular ideology – what everyone expects you to believe – and what the true story really is out there.

So do your research and get ready. Figure out whether you're going to stay where you are or move away and what to expect. If you do move, consider a state without state income taxes or with less stringent divorce requirements or cheaper lawyers or better-looking women. If you can get out, get out early … before the axe falls on your steady income.

Try to figure out if there's a way of protecting your earnings. We talked about hiding money you've already made, but what about the income? If you're a straight paycheck kind of guy, you might also be known as a sitting duck kind of guy. Everyone knows what you make! What your wife doesn't grab, your lawyer will.

Take a minute to think about your career. Can you make some moves right now? Go out on your own? Get some consulting work? Design a new kind of software or something? Can you do something to bring in money that your wife doesn't know about? If you begin now, she doesn't find out until your lawyer shows her your taxes next April. If you get money in November, deposit it in January. She won't see it until April of the following year. Try to get yourself off of that single source of income.

Let's pause for a moment with the IRS. Take a deep breath. Hold it forever. Hah, hah. Just kidding.

As we all know, every dumped wife in America calls the IRS. Scorned women are on the phone to them every hour of every day. Needless to say, they don't go after every guy who files for divorce. *They only go after the guys who cheat on their taxes.* If you don't cheat on your taxes, forget it. The IRS won't listen unless your wife has proof. And a few little phony deductions for business meals don't make the grade. She's going to need evidence that you stuffed your scuba tanks with cash last year and hauled it all down to the Caribbean. Or you have a cash 'n carry business operating in your basement in the middle of the night. It has to be serious and it has to be provable. The feds rarely go after people who are suspected of having less than a quarter million in hidden money. And even then, it's a big hassle for them. Yes, they love a tip from an ex-wife if it's the real thing. But if you haven't cheated on your taxes, and I mean really cheated, they won't give her the time of day.

Now maybe this is cold comfort to you, and, if so, I suggest you move to Sri Lanka right away. Or get yourself some hiking boots and set off for Tibet, never to return. The IRS will get you eventually if she's really got the goods on you, so don't wait around for that knock on your door. So much for tax evasion.

Make yourself a highball, sit down, and relax. There's more.

There's another little-known fact about the IRS that your lawyer will probably decide not to tell you: Your wife's lawyer cannot subpoena the IRS. There are privacy laws protecting your taxes, and the IRS will not give your records to your wife, her lawyer, or the court. Of course, as soon as you decide to leave her, you'll file separately. Then it's your call whether or not she sees your taxes. Either you cooperate with your wife, her lawyer, and her judge, or you sit in the can a few days or you run or you just stonewall them. They can't get your tax returns from the IRS unless the feds decide to investigate you, and that won't happen without solid evidence of tax evasion. And that's not the same crime as dumping your wife. Nice to know there are still a few prerogatives left for men in this world. Of course, you can't get her tax returns either, but who cares?

Let's get back to the problem of your income. What if you have a professional practice? You're a doctor, an accountant, an architect, for example. Your partners aren't going to be too thrilled when your wife starts going through your whole business. She and her lawyers will want to paw through your records, your bank accounts, your payroll, your secretary's calendar. And for what? To sniff things out. To figure what she's entitled to. That, folks, is the key word: Entitlement. The judge will go right along with it too.

What about your partners? Oh, they'll probably put up with a certain amount of harassment; then, they'll start getting on your ass. You'll be better off if you can think about breaking away. Or maybe your colleagues will survive the onslaught. It depends on what kind of wife you have. Is DESTRUCTION at the top of her list of things to do? If so, get ready for tough problems at the office. And you might be moving, right? If you decide to move, get out *before* things go bad. She'll have less power and less access to the business if you're not there anymore. Maybe you can work something out with your colleagues before you go. A little deal for your clients or patients or whatever. Your present clients might desert you anyway when your wife calls to tell them what a disgusting slimebag you are. You might need a fresh start. Think about it now. In advance.

All of this is to say, guard your income. Guard your money and your livelihood. You don't know how bad it can get. I met one guy in Illinois whose whole company was given to his ex-wife in a court-ordered settlement. His whole company! The rewards for being dumped can be very generous these days. You need to re-think your entire situation. It's your life and your business. This is part of the nuts and bolts preparation you must do. Take as much time as you need.

Anticipate the worst.

Always, in a divorce, anticipate the worst. It might not be that bad and you might say, this book is out in left field. I hope, for your sake, you do say that one day. But, just in case, you better be prepared. Get the research done. Prepare your business or your job for an incredible onslaught. Get yourself together. Exercise. Be strong. Prepare to unload.

Chapter Eight

Breaking The News & The Big Bribe

You've been waiting for this moment. If you have a girl-friend, she's *really* been waiting for it. It has a sense of significance. You're making a move. Breaking the news. Taking the first step towards a new life.

So far, we've discussed three types of wives. Yours may not be one of these. But chances are, she's some kind of combination of a One, Two, or Three. There are two kinds of wives who are not discussed here. One of them is the kind who wants to dump you. No comment. And another is the reasonable kind of wife who knows and understands that your marriage is no good and also wants it to end. That would be heaven. You could practically stay married to her just for that! Things just aren't working out and to her, like you, it's just a matter of logistics and maybe a little sadness at this point.

There they are again, the lucky bunch! People like that actually exist. They're out there somewhere enjoying their lives, I guess. But you didn't marry one of the good ones. Bummer. Not lucky. Maybe next time.

Remember one thing: You're not alone. For the vast unlucky majority of men, what do we have on the menu? Let's see, we have a virtual smorgasbord of unsavory female dishes:

1. **Wife One**: Passive, dependent, head-in-the sand woman who seems calm and meek but you never know when she's going to reach for that revolver;

2. **Wife Two**: Conniving, ladder-climbing, wild woman who has always dreamed of destroying you anyway;

3. **Wife Three**: Self-absorbed, self-righteous career woman with lots of friends and her own agenda.

Each one will take the news in a different way. You've got to try to anticipate her and be ready with whatever reaction you're going to need.

Wife One doesn't want to know. Don't tell me! Go ahead and screw around. My head is in the sand. I just want to be married. Let me be. Sob, sob. Hiccup. What will I do? I'll never survive without you. How could you do this to me? What about the children? You're ruining our lives. On and on.

You can break the news to Wife One in the privacy of your own home. She will probably not pick up a kitchen knife and heave it at your chest. (But you can't be sure, man, so stay alert. Wife One may have latent tendencies of violence that have been suppressed for years. They could make their debut on the day you leave her. Just watch out for sneaky moves. Wife One is very lonely, and that makes her sneaky.)

For the most part, though, Wife One will probably control herself. She'll cry a lot and give you those sad puppy-dog eyes. The guilt will settle over you like a wet blanket. Even though you'll feel bad, it's a good thing. It means that Wife One still loves you. She wants to stay married, and she's in a reaction mode. It will take Wife One quite a long time before she goes to the lawyer. Other people will exert a heavy influence on her. She'll have to be dragged to the lawyer by her "well-meaning" friends. Once there, however, she'll attack like any other dumped wife – with fangs.

But they're not in the picture now. You are. And Wife One still loves you. The goal, then, is to get to her before the lawyers do. You're still her number one hero. You have the biggest influence on her right now. You have a chance at the Big Bribe.

Here's the introduction. I'm not happy. I've tried. I still love you and always will, but I have to leave. I just can't stay here anymore. I don't know what's wrong with me, but I do know that I need some time to myself. No. There isn't anyone else. It's me. I have to be alone for a while. You've always been so understanding. Let's try to get through this together … blah, blah, blah. You know the drill. After you've had a few of these self-flagellating, heart-to-heart talks with Wife One, try the Big Bribe.

Here it is. We don't want to lose everything to lawyers, do we? We don't want to drag our lives through the courts. I'll always love you and take care of you. Let's just sign the papers for divorce and I'll give you the house and the car and all of our (insert your assets here, whatever they are, 'cause she's going to get them anyway). I'll give you any-thing you want. I promise I'll take care of you and the kids until I die.

Be sure to have the cheap-o divorce agreement in your hand for her to sign. Be prepared! You can get boilerplate no-fault divorce papers that don't contain any stipulations about custody, payments, or any of that garbage. Go to a low-rent storefront law office. Foreign immigration lawyers are a great source for cheap-o legal papers. (Don't tell your real lawyer or dollar signs will pop out of his eyeballs.) Have the papers ready for her when she's at her weakest, lowest point. Get her to sign. Say anything, do anything – just make her sign! If your state forces you to go to a notary, then go to one on the other side of town. Take her out to lunch afterwards. Buy her some jewelry or something. Just make her sign.

This is the Big Bribe. It's BIG because it will save you thousands of dollars. Thousands. Whatever you do, don't haggle over anything! If you have any doubts about whether or not you should do this, read the chapter on lawyers right now.

Face it. You're going to lose it anyway. You might as well give it away and get something out of it. That's right. Free-dom's not free. But you're getting an incredibly good deal. You're getting a divorce with no strings attached. Millions of men would tear their hair out in jealousy if they heard about it. Give her whatever she wants, for godssakes. You'll have more control over her and over your kids. You'll be free of court orders and lawyers. This is divorce heaven, man. If you think you can pull it off, go for it!

There's a good chance that the Big Bribe will work with Wife One. She hasn't yet discovered her own destructive powers. She may not be aware that the tide of ideology has given her powers beyond her own imagination, that just being a woman is all it takes these days to get a little "justice." Get her while she's still stuck in the "I'm a married lady" frame of mind because, you see, when they walk into court, Wives One, Two, and Three, all have the same amount of clout. They don't even have to roar anymore. All they have to do is walk in the door.

There's a small chance that Wife Three will take the Big Bribe, too. She may worry about her own salary and think, mistakenly, that she'll actually have to pay you something. Or she might get all insecure about her reputation. Or maybe she's cheap *and* greedy, and she doesn't want to pay a lawyer, and she thinks that your marital belongings are worth it. She might do it if you say the magic words: *You can have everything.* Try it. Look into a mirror and say these words out loud: *You can have everything.* Practice it a few times. Try to make her sign the papers. Have them ready, along with some heavy-duty sweet talk. You don't have to read it, honey. Such a boring document. We don't need this divorce business in our lives. We're too sophisticated for that, aren't we? Let's just take care of this and then you'll see that I don't want anything from you. What's mine is yours. It's as simple as that. Whip out a dozen roses and say anything to make her sign it. I'll even leave my CD collection here. Get the picture? Hand her a pen. Take her out to dinner. Even if it doesn't work, it's worth a try.

If you're worrying about your CDs, your designer furniture, or your autographed baseball collection, get this, buddy: Forget it. Let her have it all. If you can get her to sign on to the Big Bribe, you're the one who is getting the good deal. If Wife Three is willing to let you go without a legal battle, just grab the papers and your coat and get your ass out of there!

Of course, any wife can go weeping into court later on and claim that you tricked her into it or that she didn't have her lawyer at her side when she signed it or whatever. Sure, she can get it changed if she spends the money and if she needs to (that is, if you don't take care of her like you said you would or if your best is never enough). Let them change it later on, if they want. The longer she lives with the Big Bribe, the harder it will be for her to get it changed. And once you're divorced, bud, you're divorced. Here's what I'm saying: Go for it.

It's doubtful, though, that Wife Three will sign at all. Unlike Wife One, she'll probably want to read the damned thing and when she does, she'll realize that she's not exactly cashing in, if you know what I mean. She'll start thinking "legal" when she reads it and she'll say, hmmmm, I can do better than this. She knows that all those lawyers at the beach house do something during the week. If she gets this far, you're finished. Forget about the Big Bribe with Wife Three.

Let's backtrack a little. Say you already know she won't go for the Big Bribe. All you want to know is how to break the news to Wife Three. Let's see. You're about to ruin her life. What can you say? You could start a big fight and yell it at her. But then she'll expect to make up. No, the best way to break the news to Wife Three is a simple, straightforward declaration at home (not in front of the kids, of course).

Naturally, her first question will be: Are you seeing someone else? Lie! If you have a girlfriend, don't admit it. If Wife Three is not ripe for the Big Bribe, don't give anything away, and that includes information. Most guys make this mistake either out of guilt or fear or love for their girlfriends. Forget it, man. You're not Cyrano de Bergerac, okay? Do not *ever* declare your love for your girlfriend to anyone at any time, except perhaps to your girlfriend herself, maybe in your memoirs when you're about to die. Okay? It's a big mistake. Don't do it.

Back to Wife Three. The questions will come at you like baseballs in a batting cage. "Are you seeing someone else?" will be the first one. Then …

"Do you have another apartment?"

"No. I'm just moving out for a while."

"How long?"

"I don't know."

Don't tell Wife Three anything except that you are moving out for a while to think about your life and your relationship. Buy time. Say anything you think she might want to hear. In other words, slip out the back door.

"Where are you going?"

"I don't know."

"Will you call?"

"Yes."

"When?"

"I don't know."

Get the picture? Questions, questions, questions. One thing you'll get used to is not answering questions. It's good practice, anyway. After all, your Wife Three could be a lawyer, herself. Remember, she's the vulnerable one right now, but that won't last long. Don't give any information away. Just go.

If you are married to Wife Two – and you've probably forced yourself to admit it by now if you are – I really feel sorry for you. You're in real trouble. On the other hand, you're about to rid yourself of someone who really hates your guts, at least on a subliminal, animalistic level. Whether or not she admits it, this woman is not loved and she blames you. It will be a relief to get away from her, no matter what it costs. You don't have to feel bad about leaving this one. She really deserves it.

Forget the Big Bribe with Wife Two. No chance. She already knows that you're leaving – she sensed it because she's so suspicious. But she doesn't know when. Timing. It's your only advantage. You have two options. You can just walk out and not even tell her. Or you can tell her in a restaurant as a way of protecting yourself against flying cleavers.

In fact, you might really *want* to tell her. Maybe, deep down, you loathe her so much that you want to have this one little moment of triumph. You're a dumped wife now, babe. Tough. Give yourself this moment of illusory pleasure if you want it. It will be your last. Or just pack up while she's not home and walk out the door. Don't leave a note!

First, try to get yourself a stretch of time when she won't be around. This is difficult with Wife Two. She's *always* around. Bide your time. When you do get your chance, clean out as much stuff as you can carry. Paw through her desk and files. Check all of her hiding places. Look for unfamiliar bank books and hidden papers that you might need later. Swipe keys. Take whatever you can from Wife Two today because it will all be hers tomorrow. To hell with the doorman and the neighbors. Rent a truck. Get everything out now because Wife Two will change the locks tomorrow.

Listen up, now, if your wife is a Wife Two. On the day that you break the news you must call all your credit card companies and report your cards stolen. This is one of the advantages of timing. Unless you've been sloppy and she knows when you're leaving, you can catch the cards before she takes the cash advances and charges them to their limits. *Call today!* Have them fax a statement to you immediately. You'll need it. What about bank overdrafts and bank credit lines? Today, on the day you leave, stop all activity on all of your joint accounts.

Here's the problem: You call up your major credit card next week and say, I've left my wife and I want to close my account. Forget it! You'll get some nameless, faceless robot telling you that you need your wife's permission to close the account. She can charge to the limit, as far as they are concerned. After all, *you're* the one who will have to pay. Equal rights? Very funny. It's still the Stone Age to them. They go after the husband and that's it. She charges; you pay.

Let's see. You have, say, five active credit cards together. Each one has a limit of five or six thousand dollars. The day you break the news (or before), Wife Two takes cash advances on all of them, plus all your bank credit line accounts and, um, what does that amount to? About $25,000 or $30,000 at 22% interest. Holy smokes! She gets the cash and you get the bills.

On the day you leave, report the cards stolen and stop all the activity. Call the banks. Stop the accounts. Then send them all notarized letters saying that you stopped the accounts on such and such a day and that you will not be responsible for charges after that date. Get the name of the clerk when you call. Try to get some kind of confirmation to refer to in your letter. You'll still have to pay all the bills, but you may save a few thousand dollars by acting fast.

Wife Two. She'll be back soon. Have you cleaned out everything you want and everything you might need? Don't get soft on her just because she's not there to badger you. Wife Two is a slow-burning deadly fire. Whatever you can get today will be all you ever get, man. You've got one chance and it's now. So break the news in a restaurant if you want, but don't tell her anything, because, just like Wife Three, she'll use each and every bit of information against you in a court of law.

They'll act like you're a criminal now. Don't give information to the prosecution just to be nice. Don't say, "I'll do my best" or "I'll take care of the kids." She'll run to them, screaming that you've deserted them, no matter what you say. Don't waste any energy on Wife Two and don't expect her to act like a human. Her worst nightmare is coming into reality; murder is not out of the question. Protect yourself. Arm yourself. This woman is at war.

Well, friend, you're on your way, for better or worse. Whatever happens now, your life will never be the same. If you have a girlfriend, you can go to your favorite little place and have a nice toast. Good for you! You've broken the news. If you don't have a girlfriend, maybe you can find someone, preferably a good-looking female who doesn't know your wife, to hang out with a little while. You deserve to celebrate.

Give yourself a little break (two days) because you've probably been pretty tense lately. Have a drink. Relax. Go to Florida for the weekend. Recharge your batteries because the battle of your life lies ahead.

But, hey, congratulations!

Chapter Nine

Lawyers & Other Scoundrels

Any time anyone says anything bad about lawyers. it is dismissed as "lawyer bashing." Then the attorneys, as they like to call themselves, go back to their conference rooms and count their chips. Isn't it funny the way lawyers rant and rave about constitutional rights, but they want to make lawyer jokes illegal? It's okay to say whatever you want – that's free speech. But make fun of a lawyer, and it's "hate speech." That cracks me up! I'm tempted to throw in a few good ones right here. Uh, oh. I better not. I might get arrested.

This chapter is not about lawyer bashing, anyway. Some lawyers are decent people, nice people, wonderful, cute and cuddly people. I guess so. Aside from all the destructive and reprehensible work that they do, they could be all right. Personally, I find it difficult to separate the person from the work, but if you're related to a lawyer, I suppose YOU could find a way.

In fact, I suspect there is probably a whole batch of lawyers out there who would like to know how to dump their wives and might be secretly reading this book. After all, lawyers have practices and assets and children, too. Why would they have to read this book? You might wonder. The answer is simple. *The law, folks, is irrelevant.* It's a joke. We watch it on TV and we say, Gee, how could something like that happen to that poor schmuck. It's so unfair. Whatever it is. Or we see some actors on a TV show acting as if they care and we think, Ahhhh, the lofty law. Ain't it great? Look at those actors. They actually seem to care.

Wake up, man! That's TV. It's not the real world and it's not "the law." So forget about clichés and fairness and logic and all of that high-school civics crap. This is divorce.

Back in the Middle Ages when people were getting excited about law because it was kind of new and it had to do with fairness and ethics, there was plenty of abuse, too. Now, in the Twenty-First Century, we know better than to expect fairness or ethics from lawyers and judges. We're left with the abuse. Bummer.

If you forget everything else in this book, you must remember one thing: *There's no one out there checking up on these guys.* They do whatever they want. And you, bud, are at their mercy. I know one guy who could have gotten a divorce in New York three years before he finally did because his lawyer "forgot to tell him" about the difference between court-ordered maintenance and voluntary maintenance. Oops. A few thousand dollars in tax deductions went down the toilet too. Oops. Maybe his lawyer didn't want the case to get resolved too quickly. What are you going to do, sue the guy?

When your divorce begins, you'll probably have the best intentions. I just want to get this over with. I'll pay what I have to pay. I'll go along with whatever the judge wants. I just want to get through it.

Sorry, Charlie. You're in for the long haul.

But have hope. This chapter can help.

First of all, have you done as much preparation as you possibly can before calling your lawyer? Did you do your research? Did you go to the library? You don't need a library card to go in and read, maybe make copies of a few things. Do you know the story in your own state? Don't rely entirely on the tables in the back of this book because they might not be up to date by the time of publication. Be prepared. Shop and compare. If you live in Massachusetts or New York, maybe you should scope out the Virgin Islands or Alaska, the last frontier. Look around and make informed decisions about where you're going and what you're going to do *before* you go to a lawyer.

Let's face it, some states are more appealing than others. Some cater to the outdoorsy type and others offer glamour, civilization, and excitement. Some states have unique business opportunities. These days you can go anywhere. Have computer and fax machine, will travel. Wherever you go, remember one thing about moving: Unless you're planning to disappear into thin air, she will still be able to get you in your new state. The long arm of the law will reach out and grab your money no matter where you go. If you move to Nevada, your wife in Illinois will still be able to haul in your dough. You might get a divorce in Kansas or Louisiana, but you'll be tied to the courts and to your assets in your home state. Moving is not simple, but it might be smart. And if you're going to get out of California, why go to a California lawyer?

Get out first. Then find your lawyer. A lawyer in your old state just makes your wife's life a lot easier.

Remember what I told you about judges? They're just lawyers who got promotions or appointments. Or they're politicians who run for office on platforms of trendy public opinion. All judges were once lawyers. This is very important because when you go into court you should know that you are facing a united front. Sure, they yell at each other. It's fun for them. They all play together. They go to the same conferences. They hang out at the same hotels in Hawaii. It's the We're-In-Charge-Of-The-World-Club and you, fella, are not invited to join.

This is the reason why it is a bad idea to represent yourself. You might be thinking, well, if these guys are such a bunch of jerks, why not just speak for myself? I have the right. I'll do it myself. It's a temptation, true. It would be nice if we folks out here had some say over what happens to us in court. Unfortunately, it doesn't work. Being your own lawyer is a big mistake. Don't do it. They hate that! And they'll hate you if you try to do their job. They have a hard enough time trying to justify their phony-baloney jobs anyway without some wise guy coming in and saying he can do it better. Yeah, yeah, you *could* do it better, but it doesn't work. The bias that is already working against you because you're a male will increase, blow up, get huge, and out of control. Why? Because they HATE to be insulted. And when you walk in and say "I can do it myself," their little feelings get hurt. Judges, especially, make important decisions based on their little feelings. The lawyers, though, will be the ones who really go after you. All kinds of little procedural tricks and secret meaningless rules will be thrown in your face to invalidate your case. These petty pickings are the stock in trade of every lawyer's daily life. He will twist and turn the jargon around you like a fat piece of taffy. Eventually, you'll get screwed.

Many men are attempting to represent themselves in divorces these days because men, in general, are getting screwed so badly. Don't do it. It's a big mistake.

Then what? How can I find a lawyer I can trust? Hmmmm. What's wrong with that question? A lawyer you can trust. That's a tall order.

Let's be real. Say your wife serves you with some papers. It's like spinning a roulette wheel. You get a judge assigned to your case. A lawyer with a robe on. You get yourself a lawyer. Don't get your brother-in-law! Don't pick your best friend who has known you since you were five. Forget it. Get someone you never met before because in a few months you're going to hate his or her guts. This cannot be helped. The lawyer's job is to drag the case on so that he or she can make money.

Consider this: Do you really want to see your friend, Billy the legal beagle, build a deck on his summer house with your money while you're scraping by? It might be hard to imagine this happening, but your friendship with Billy the beagle will be tough enough to handle, even if he's not your lawyer (see Chapter Eleven).

The bottom line is, it doesn't really matter who you get as long as you get someone you don't know. Lawyers are journeymen, functionaries. They're given a set of procedures and told to follow them. Law school doesn't exactly attract loads of creative people. And those who are creative don't make the best lawyers (because they probably never wanted to be lawyers in the first place. So if your lawyer displays even a spark of creativity, check to make sure she's not writing her big mystery novel and billing you for the time.).

Lawyers drag through the day, going through the paces, carrying around big cases, filled with the debris of your marriage. They complain a lot. They make too much money. There are thousands of them out there, and thousands more are pouring out of law school looking for the big bucks. Where are they coming from? From you! And where are the creative ideas going to come from? Also from you. Not from them. Lawyers make a bunch of rules, and then they follow them. Expect a bowling alley attendant in a suit. Procedure is everything. The law itself is irrelevant.

Your lawyer will demand a retainer of anywhere from $1000 to $40,000 (or more) depending on the kind of clothes you're wearing when you meet him, what his office rent is like, and where you live. When you interview your lawyer, he'll interview you. All he wants to know is how much money you have. He might ask you a bunch of questions about your wife and kids, but what he wants to know is what you make, what your apartment or house is worth, what you have in the bank. Be careful! You're not under oath so don't cut your nuts off. Tread lightly.

The lawyer is not going to take you on, give you tons of good legal advice, move your case forward, and act in your best interest. How the hell can he make any money if he does that? You'd be settled and divorced before he could say "Porsche Cayenne." On the other hand, there's nothing you can do about this.

The best thing you can do is to offer your wife a settlement right away. Up front. This way, two years and thousands of dollars later, you can say, "Hey, I made a great offer when I had some real money." Keep making offers. Make it look like she won't settle. No matter what is happening in the court, keep the offers coming. Make them realistic, too. Remember, no one is going to want to let you off the hook. Try to look good on paper. Change a number here or there and send in a new one every few months.

Your lawyer will not want to do this and she will probably advise you to hold your offers back. She may even refuse to send them in. Why? She wants to prolong the case. She wants to put her face in front of the judge again and again because lawyers love to do this. It gets them known. Oh, I know that judge, she'll tell her next client. I just had a three-year case with him. We're old friends. Great. If the next guy takes any comfort from hearing that, he better read this book too!

Another sad but true thing to face right now is that your lawyer is on your wife's side. Either he's saddled with a horse himself or he simply buys into the whole biased group feeling that leaving one's wife is bad news. Or, maybe your lawyer is a woman who thinks, "Oh, my god, what if my husband dumps me? What if he walks out on me? Me, me, me, me!!!"

Again, there's not much you can do about this. It's human nature. Try to avoid lawyers who like to talk about themselves a lot, have opinions, or seem to have any feelings at all. Your best bet would be a real Kafkaesque bureaucrat who will shuffle into court and mumble a lot.

You think I'm joking? I'm serious!

Eventually, when your lawyer gets so bad that you can't stand the sound of his voice on your machine or her smirk when she says, "I'm sure the judge will throw you in jail if you don't hand over your IRA by tomorrow," change lawyers. But beware. You'll be expected to pay off the last one and come up with another retainer for the new one. It's part of the program: Abuse.

You might be thinking that if you hire an expensive, high-powered lawyer that somehow you'll be better off or in good hands or something. It's another trap. Unless you happened to be descended from the robber barons of the nineteenth century and your family already controls the courts, it won't do you any good. In fact, it will hurt your case. Why? The wife's lawyer will make a big deal about how much you're paying. You're so rich! Your expensive lawyer will make you look wealthy while he gradually relocates your net worth into his pocket. Do you really want to pay for the view from his office? Do you want to pay for a covey of secretaries, those state-of-the-art computers, and five-dollar copies?

The fact is that a cheap, fast-food-type lawyer will have the same papers about you coming across his desk, the same little rules to follow, the same work to do. As a matter of fact, a quiet, low-key lawyer might actually send in your settlement proposals if you ask him to do it. And he might not be cocky enough to hang around the courthouse blabbing with his friends, charging you for it.

Be careful, though. Cheap lawyers who can be bossed around are very hard to find. Most lawyers are given ego-expansion drugs in law school which soon become a powerful addiction. Try a chain-store-type law office where the lawyers get a salary and act a little embarrassed about working there. Or visit your local courthouse and observe a few civil cases. If you see someone you think you can stand, ask him for his card.

Be sure to interview your lawyer twice. For one thing, lawyers have been rather uptight about their image lately. Gee, I wonder why. These days they're trying to improve it, and they've been telling each other to listen to clients more. Some of them actually do it during the first interview. So, again, beware.

If you go to a lawyer who sits quietly and listens to you and asks a few relevant questions, go back. Talk to him or her again. The second time will reveal the truth. Either she'll listen again, take some notes, and appear to be a real possibility or she'll turn into a human Tower of Babble right before your very eyes! Hey, what happened to the quiet interest? The courteous questions? Suddenly you're slammed in the face with a bunch of meaningless jargon, useless anecdotes, lectures on the law, and all kinds of other farm-like substances until you rush out the door into the fresh air. Whew! Thank god you didn't hand over your retainer on the first visit.

Sooner or later, you'll get yourself someone you can stand. There are so many lawyers out there that you will be able to find one to suit your needs. What's the next step? Pay your money, of course. In addition to paying your lawyer, you'll spend all your time with your lawyer talking about what you have to pay.

"I'll pay!" "I'll pay!" you might say. And pay, you will. That's great. Unfortunately, it won't be enough. Do you mean, you'll be willing to pay 25-50% more than you make? Double what you have in the bank? Your wife's lawyer is advising her to inflate her demands. She knows you don't have twice what you have or make three times what you make. Yeah, you know she knows. But that's reality. It's not the law. So pay three times what you're able to pay, okay? Any problem with that? It's a difficult thing for most men to achieve. You've probably heard that many men file for bankruptcy during or after a divorce. Supposedly, they're all trying to avoid paying alimony and child support. The real reason is that they're cleaned out. Sucked dry. Declaring bankruptcy can't help a divorce victim anyway. That's history. And the missed payments or the money you can't send adds up. They call it arrears, and they use it to get you if you ever do have any money. Meanwhile, the demands are way out of line and everyone knows it. But no one cares.

If you get a judge who thinks you're a piece of rancid meat for daring to leave your fantastic wife, he or she can order you to pay any amount, regardless of what you make or have. Guidelines? Rules? Laws? Cough, cough. Very funny. They make up the rules as they go along. They can order you to pay any number they pick out of a hat. Remember: There's no one checking up on these guys. They do whatever they want.

So if your lawyer wants you to give him every piece of paper in your office, every cancelled check from the past five years, every bank statement you've got, think twice. For one thing, you probably won't ever get the stuff back. They need all that junk to fill up their over-sized briefcases and make pretend that they're working. Sure, they work. They lug your papers around. But you can pay someone a lot less to do that, if you want.

Back to the laugh track. Yes, they want everything on you, net worth statements every few months, your phone records, your passport, your fifth-grade diary. They want it all. Wait a minute. Didn't you misplace your passport? What happened to those cancelled checks? You must weigh the subtle advantages of the appearance of cooperation against your control of the information. If the judge hates you because of your chromosomes right off the bat, then why seek to appease her? Being a man is a bad way to start out in court. Maybe you can keep your nose clean by giving "the appearance of cooperation." That means that you *think* before you hand something over to your lawyer. You *think carefully* before you offer up your heart and soul for the judge to slice up into little pieces. And if you're wondering how much to tell your lawyer, who wants to know everything, remember that once you tell anyone something, another person knows it. Here's a guideline: Tell your lawyer everything and anything that your wife already knows. Let him hear it from you first. It gives him a feeling of control. That's nice. Let him have his feelings, while you keep control.

They'll threaten you with prison. They might send you to prison. Just think about it. Your wife, her lawyer, and her judge would *love* to see you in jail. Respected businessman, doctor, architect – Book 'em, Danno. This is the chief threat that they hold over you, besides taking all of your money, of course. Prison. Jail. Your own lawyer will be the first to tell you that it's a real possibility.

So what's so bad about prison? A few epidemics floating around. Some hard-core murderers. Tough drug addicts. Rats, human and otherwise. Prison. Sure, you can think of places you'd rather go, but if you don't do exactly what the judge tells you to do, that's where you'll end up – temporarily.

It's a real problem. The problem comes when the judge orders you to do things that you simply can't do, such as pay a rock star's yearly salary to your wife. And what are you supposed to live on? Remorse? Whoa. Hang in there. Don't give up. Bad as it might be, divorce is just an expensive journey through our illustrious justice sewer, I mean, system.

All right, you say, I can handle it. But who is that squirrelly-looking guy in the old Chrysler hanging around me?

Hey, that's your wife's private investigator. He's taking pictures of you and your girlfriend or you and your dates. He wants to help your wife establish fault. She'll get more money from the judge if she can catch you in the act. If you have a few dates, don't worry about it. The judge is going to assume that you're a scumbag anyway if you leave your wife. A few assorted beauties will only liven up the judge's fantasy life for a day. But if you have a real girlfriend, be very careful. You don't want Wife-o-Raptor to find out about your true love at this point.

The investigator isn't doing much, though. He's running your social security number through a database to find out all about your bank accounts in the state. Taping your phone calls? Probably. Checking into your female friends? For sure! Who are they? Where do they come from? Oooh. Just like in the movies. Strange calls may come in from your credit card companies and banks who get all mixed up when investigators inquire. What was that you wanted to know, Mr. So-and-So, about your margin account? It gets to be a pain in the neck. Your secretary might get some calls under false pretenses, like this:

"Hi, I'm Sherry and I'm a friend of Joe's (you) from college. And I wondered, does he have a trip planned to the Cayman Islands? Does he ever go to the Poconos without his wife?" Etc.

It won't be this obvious, but if your secretary is the nosy type, she might just play along to find out what's going on. Who knows what she knows? Or what she'll say. *There's only one way to guard information, and that's to keep it to yourself.*

The investigator will keep demanding more and more money from your wife. She has to pay him up front and the price usually starts at around $8000 or $9000 for the basic works. Eventually, the guy in the old Chrysler will drive off when the wife has paid all she wants to pay. In the meantime, be careful. Check your apartment for bugs and micro-cameras. Call your girlfriend from pay phones. You know the drill. You're being very careful these days anyway, right?

Lawyers. Scoundrels. They're out there, all right. Out to get you. Or maybe you're a lawyer and you're reading this with disgust, but you want to dump your wife, too. Are you a matrimonial lawyer? If so, I wish you the best of luck with your family law colleagues.

If you're another kind of lawyer, tax or corporate or medical malpractice or something, you still have to hire a matrimonial lawyer to handle your case. You still have to do your own research. And you're still going to be at the mercy of a judge who will see you not as a lawyer, but as a scumbag-husband deserting his poor wife. Maybe the judge will go easy on you because you're a member of the club. Maybe not. I don't know what kind of advantage it will give you up front, but your income and your practice, your law degree and your kids are still at the mercy of the man or the woman on the bench. You are going to have to be on your guard as much as any guy. Beware of yourself. Don't get cocky. Use your contacts and your freebies, whatever they might be, but keep your eye on the ball.

Doctor, lawyer, chief financial officer – everyone's floating in the same boat, spinning in the same cultural whirlpool. Hold on.

Chapter Ten

Begging & Pleading

At some point, in between "I'm leaving" and the final decree, you will have to grapple with this big question: Should I go back? Your wife is begging you. Your kids are pleading with you. Maybe your girlfriend turned out to be less than fantastic. She wasn't as great, loyal, strong, loving, or generally terrific as you thought she was at first. Or maybe you've been out on the town and you've had a few dates that make marriage to anyone look like an oasis compared to the gang-warfare of single life. Should I go back? This lawyer stuff is getting to me. My money is running out fast. My kids cry whenever I see them. I'm ruining everyone's life. Should I go back? Should I? HELP!

There's still time to go back. Your wife may have kept a few of your clothes in the closet, hoping that it will turn out to be a "family crisis" rather than a full-blown divorce. "Hoping" is hardly the word! She's begging and pleading. She's threatening suicide. She's sending the kids out on missions. Make him come back! She's writing letters. She's calling your office, calling her friends, calling your friends.

She's calling you night and day. Crying. Wailing. Begging to see you, just for lunch or a drink or an innocent cup of coffee. Let's talk, she says. Give me another chance. Little Joey threw up in school yesterday. Teenage Erica is doing drugs. They're all flunking out of school. I've lost twenty pounds (finally). The house is on fire! The dog is dead. Help us, please! Come home. We need you. We love you. We're your family. I'll do anything to make you happy. Come back. Come back. Come back, please!

Well? What are you going to do?

The guys who bought this book for fun or out of curiosity will be the first to troop in, heads bowed, shoulders rounded. The other guys who thought their girlfriends were true blue but turned out not to be, they'll be next. They'll settle for the wife rather than face the world alone. Yeah, they'll shuffle in the back door. And the last bunch, the ones who would rather put up with that "inmate" feeling day after day rather than face the certain loss of their kids (a big one), the trauma of divorce, and the destruction of all life on earth as they know it, they'll be along any day now.

This is the time when convictions go soft, when the little apartment with the futon on the floor doesn't seem like your real life at all. This is the time when you think, hey, I tried it. I went out on my own for a few weeks or months. I gave it a go and, well, it wasn't for me. I noticed that I'm calling the old house "home" again. Yeah, I am. It doesn't look so bad from a distance and I miss the comforts. I do. You know, I worked hard to pay for that house and everything in it. I walk away and what have I got? A girlfriend? A few dates and frozen dinners?

If you lose your conviction and decide to go back, just remember one thing: Your kids will be comforted and relieved. If you leave them again, they get a double dose of pain. So don't take your kids on a roller-coaster ride of indecision. It's worse for them than getting used to divorce. It puts them in limbo – not a nice place for kids to be. So make up your mind and, if you go back, just hunker down for the long haul.

What about the rest? What about the men who really want to dump their wives? Who want to survive the begging and pleading and get on with their lives? You guys, read on.

Let's take another look at our wives in all their glory.

Wife One, ostrich-head, begs and pleads for a long time in an earnest way. She still loves you. She'll take you back, no matter what. She wants to stay married more than anything in the world, even if you ignore her and practically live with your girlfriend. She'll settle for anything, do anything to avoid divorce.

Once she finds out how to get in touch with you, she'll be on the phone begging and pleading. You have to give her your number because you need to see or, at least, talk to your kids. Plus, she's not a bad woman. You said you'd be there for her and you will be. Did she take the Big Bribe? You don't want to be cruel. Firm is one thing; mean is another. She's not a bad person and, chances are, she's showing you her worst side and the kids her best.

There is real hope here for some communication and cooperation after the initial shock wears off. The longer you stay in the picture, the better. Friends and lawyers will pressure her, but your influence will be stronger. It makes sense to be there for Wife One. Don't fly out the door never to return. It's a balance. You're not there and you are getting divorced; yet you care. Show up now and then. Stay in touch. Try to keep things on an even keel. If she starts to freak out, lay low for a few days. Then come back and take control of the situation. It's a balancing act with Wife One.

Let's skip Wife Two and proceed to Three for now. Wife Three is all upset. She's thinking: That son of a bitch, how dare he walk out on me! He'll be sorry. Who does he think he is? How dare he!

Then it sinks in. Single again. No way, she says. No way. She calls you up and says, Let's see a counselor. Couples therapy. You've got to give it a try. We can't afford divorce. It will ruin the children's lives. You have a moral obligation to try to work it out. I've made an appointment, blah, blah, blah. Look at Steve and Sherry, Marvin and Debbie, Oren and Chloe, and on and on. Wife Three does not want to go the way of Linda, 40, Julia, 38, Maria, 42, Colette, 52, Diane, 39 … She knows they're miserable. At least I already have kids, she thinks. Thank god for that. But I don't want to go out on dates. I don't want to lose my beach house! I don't want to be like those wildly desperate women hunting for men. Help! Come back. Let's work it out.

Go to a couple of sessions with the (kook) therapist just to show good faith. Be realistic. Your kids will pressure you. The therapist, who thrives on making miserable people stay together, will pressure you. And Wife Three, in dread of the single life, will pour it on. Be careful! While you're appeasing them with your token efforts, don't give away any information.

The questions will be mixed right into the begging and pleading and, of course, into the so-called therapy. It's really an inquisition. You mean that you enjoy living alone, Mister So-and-So? Aren't you living with Ms. So-and-So from your company? What do you do on the weekends? Are you happy in your job? Is your job the same? What about the consulting that you're doing on the side? How is that going?

The questions will come at you fast and furious because this is not real therapy. This is a trap. Here's one:

"Do you miss your children?"

"Yes."

"Do you want to see them more often?"

"Yes."

"Do you want them to live with you?"

"Uhh …"

Watch out! Trap. Think: custody, court, evidence. You'll be seeing this therapist again in a little wooden booth next to the judge in about a year. He said he didn't want the children, Your Honor. Big smile. What a professional! Beware. Whatever you say to Wife Three must first pass through the meat grinder of imagined future litigation.

Yes, she wants you back. Wife Three believes in therapy. When it fails, she'll blame you. You only have a short period in which to look good on paper before the real expensive paper begins to build up. And, frankly, looking good doesn't get you very far in court these days. You are the man; you are, therefore, the beast.

Wife Three will be begging and pleading, but not for long. If you don't lead her on, she'll make a beeline for the lawyer's office. Ask yourself, is there anything I want from Wife Three? If so, now is the time to go for it. The begging and pleading period is a good time to get back into the house to pick up things that you might have forgotten or to get her signature on something if you need it. Think it through. This is the last time you'll have real access before the lawyers wall her off.

Okay, it's unavoidable. We have to talk about Wife Two. She's thinking: I knew it! I knew he'd walk out on me the minute he met some young bimbo. He'll be back. I'll just cast one of his little kids out like bait on a rod and reel him in. The big, fat fish. He'll be back. He'll pay for this. That stupid old fool. I knew it!

Wife Two begins her reign of terror with a flourish. Forget begging and pleading. You're in for screaming and howling, non-stop. Big time. Think you're safe? Wife Two has your number. She's right outside your door. Surprise! Even though she never bothered to earn a dime in her life, she now has a full-time job, and it's called pursuing and harassing you.

Nevertheless, you have to talk to your kids, or at least let them know how to reach you. Everyone is calling your office at once. Holy smokes! Twenty, thirty calls a day? You'll get fired. If you work for yourself, you'll never get any work done in a day. Come on. You can't take these calls at work. Can your secretary handle it? Can you do something to your phone? How will your kids get through to you? Maybe you need voice mail. At home, you could definitely use some kind of a state-of-the-art caller ID that lets your kids get through, but somehow screens out Wife Two. No matter where she calls from. Why? You'll see.

I'll kill myself! I'll kill the children. You scum. You sickening pig. We're starving to death. Eating out of garbage cans. Timmy and Tanya are sick. They're in the hospital.

They're diseased. Ahhhhh! How can you do this to us? We're dying. The children are dying.

The calls pour in. The notes, the letters, the telegrams, the FedEx packages. Your office is on alert. Your doorman and neighbors begin to notice. Pictures of dead children. Your own children's pictures with pins in their eyes. Sick. Really sick. Dead flowers are sent to your office.

Wife Two never lets up. The poor children. The poor dog. Come back. We're in such pain.

She calls all day. She gets your unlisted secret home number somehow and calls all night. She calls your girlfriend, goes to her office, sends her some dead flowers, too. She calls you constantly. You have to go to school with the kids. To the doctor. To the dentist. You must come back. Your parents called. Your uncle from Canada.

At night, she wails. She'll turn on the gas if you hang up. She's buying a gun tomorrow. She's planning to shoot the kids and herself. She'll put a plastic bag over Susie's head. She'll shoot little Tommy right now! They're destroyed. They're sitting on the concrete in front of the house begging for food. Come back. Come back.

Wife Two has a plan. She's thinking: I'll drive him crazy. I'll get that son-of-a-bitch back here if it's the last thing I do. I'm a married woman. I'll never give him a divorce. Never. He owes me everything. I made him what he is today. I did everything for him. He can't leave me here. I deserve to be married. I'll never let him go. Never, never, never! I'll kill him first. Why should he be happy when I'm a miserable, unloved woman? It's not fair! It's all his fault. I'll destroy him, I swear. He'll never have a day of peace as long as I'm alive!

Holy smokes, man. Wife Two. Whatever you go through, you know you did the right thing. You're not going back to that woman. No way. She's showing her true colors now, isn't she? You knew she was bad news, but this is too much. Whoa. Who would believe it? You're the only one who knows how bad she really is. No one would believe it. She behaves like a normal person in public. Unbelievable.

You should keep tapes of her suicide threats, her foul language, murder threats, all of it. Keep the disgusting cards, the poison pen letters to your colleagues, the manipulated hate mail from your kids. Stuff it in a drawer. It might not be useful, but you never know. You might get a break one day and get to show it to the judge. Keep all of it.

The sad part is the kids. They're hostages now. Maybe you can see them at school or something. Chances are, she's got them locked up. When you do see them, they're well prepped. On a mission. Totally brainwashed. You're amazed to hear the vile insults and accusations that your wife always hurls at you coming out of the mouth of your eight-year-old kid. He never talked that way before. Sad, but true. It's going to be painful to watch the way Wife Two manipulates your kids for her selfish reasons. Unfortunately, there's not much you can do about it.

As far as Wife Two herself is concerned, just shut her out. Pick up the phone and let it dangle off the edge of the table. She's a wild, wounded, vicious animal. Stay away. Don't give her any ammunition. No information. You can try to get to your kids, but remember that she'll pump them for every word you say when they get home. Don't put the burden of "not telling your mother" on them. Just don't tell them anything that you don't want her to hear.

Do not answer any letters or put anything in writing. Don't take calls from so-called friends. (We'll talk about them in Chapter Eleven.) Don't let anyone near you except for your girlfriend, if you have one. If you don't have a girlfriend, see new people. Stay out late. Pour yourself into your work. Wife Two? Steer clear of her. Shut her out.

You can't plug up a volcano.

All you can do is run from it.

If your wife was one of those strange and rare people who says, "What? You're leaving? Oh, dear. Well, I guess it's over. Good-bye," what would you do? Would you throw your arms around her and squeeze her to death out of pure joy? If only you had a great wife, if only …

It's up to you to figure out why you bought this book in the first place and why you've come this far. As we discussed before, if you're really going to leave her, don't go back for a little while and confuse your kids. If you can't manage it and you're not going to dump your wife, just face it. You're stuck, man. Yep. You're trapped in the great foulfaced sharp-toothed rat trap that a marriage becomes when it goes bad. Bummer for you.

I'm rooting for the guys who have the guts to go all the way. Grab that ball and take off down the field. You'll be the one dancing in the end zone when it's all over. Sure, the begging and pleading is hard to get through. But you can do it. Put your head down and push!

Take it in stride and you'll get past it all into a future that will be tough, but at least it will be free. A chance for real freedom, maybe even true love. Keep running and pushing and tolerating the intolerable, and one day you will be free. Go for it, man. Go now.

Chapter Eleven

Friends You Once Had

"Is Divorce Contagious?" was a recent headline on the cover of a popular woman's magazine. Watch out, girls. Divorce is going around – like a bad flu. If your friend's husband dumps her, will yours dump you?

They're scared or, shall we say, terrified of losing their husbands. So, when your "couple" friends hear that you've given the old wife the big heave, they'll react ... and not necessarily the way you expected.

Take, for example, your friends Mike and Sheryl. You've known them since you got married, or before. Mike's your good friend. Sheryl and your wife are like this: two fingers twisted. You've traveled together, or maybe shared a summer house, or your kids play together, or you always watch the Superbowl together or something. You get the picture.

Well, goodbye Sheryl ... *and* Mike. As soon as Sheryl hears the news, she tightens the rope around Mike's neck. He can barely breathe. Secretly, he blames you. You're free. He's trapped. Now, he's really behind bars because Sheryl is watching him like a starved hawk.

Maybe Mike will rebel and meet you for a drink on the sly. Still, he can't help wondering how you did it. You show him this book. But it's just a book, he claims. What about wifey-poo? What about the kids? Here it comes: How could you do it? (You scumbag, you disgusting pig.) I'm your friend, but I don't approve of this, man. Get your act together and go back. (I want everything to stay the same. How am I going to be friends with just you? You're wrecking our nice arrangement.) You really ought to go back.

They'll all tell you to think about going back. If you have a girlfriend, they might put her down. It would be better if no one knew about your girlfriend, but sometimes these things can't be helped. Your friends will feel torn. Their loyalties are confused. They don't want to choose between you and your wife. They want you to go back.

All except for your single friends. Those guys. They'll warn you about girlfriends and dates. It's a jungle out there! All women are after money. Paranoid single men. They wish some beautiful women *would* go after their money, right?

There is one line that you will hear from everyone, I mean, everyone you know. The poor kids. This is really hurting them. Yeah, sure. As if they give a crap about your kids! Listen to the next friend who says this. What he means is, maybe I can allow you to leave your wife, but I can't condone your abandonment of your children. I'm superior to you. I care about all the little children of the world. You don't. In other words, you deserve to die, you selfish beast. This is simply a golden opportunity for everyone to put you down and the best way for them to do it is by "worrying" about your kids.

Don't let them stab you with their dirty little guilt knives and get away with it. And don't think they care about your kids, either. You don't see them offering to pay next year's tuition, do you? They're not taking your kids on shopping sprees or ski weekends, are they? Nope. And why should they? Your kids are not their kids. This is a put-down, pure and simple. Take it for what it is. Give it right back, too.

Gee, good friend, how kind of you to voice your concern about my children. I had no idea that you cared about my kids so much. That's so sincere. You're such a caring person. Have you ever thought of becoming one of those poorly paid social workers who devotes his life to the welfare of children? You are such a kind-hearted individual. I wonder why I never noticed it in all these years?

Really lay it on. You'll be sorry if you don't when you get home and find yourself in a rage. This is the most common insult you'll get from your friends. What they're saying is that you don't care about your kids. You haven't given any thought to their welfare. You're dumping your children without a care in the world for their future. This friend of yours isn't judging you or anything. Oh, no. He's only concerned about the poor, helpless children because, clearly, you don't give a damn what happens to them.

How insulting can you get! It's the kind of insult that doesn't hit until a few hours after your friend has gone home, feeling superior, having spoken his mind. Soon you're in a rotten mood. You're steaming up. This person claims to be your friend? Don't bother to call back and tell him about all the heart-wrenching hours you've spent agonizing over your kids. Don't bother to tell him how you plan to give them every cent you ever make until you die. Don't bother. This friend is either seething with jealousy or is so superficial that you'd be wasting your time either way. He wants to insult you, and that's exactly what he's doing.

You're going to have to defend yourself again and again against hostile lawyers and judges. You shouldn't have to defend yourself to your own friends.

So-called friends. Unfortunately, it will be hard to take. A sad thing. It's nice to have friends. If you have a girlfriend, it will be easier. Maybe you'll like her friends. But, if you're on your own, you might get a little lonely.

Hey, what about my friend, Billy, the legal beagle? He'll help me. I've known him since high school and he's a successful lawyer now. He'll give me some advice. Let's get together for a beer. How 'bout it? Sounds good. Talk, talk, talk. But something's wrong. Funny, Billy doesn't seem to know anything about your divorce, your judge, your jurisdiction (even if he practices across the street from you), your lawyer, your rights, your chances, your strategies, your life. He simply doesn't know. He doesn't do *that* kind of law, you see. Even if he passed the bar in your state and has handled a hundred cases exactly like yours, surprise! He couldn't say one way or another whether you should do this or that.

See, lawyers don't give it away, not even to their good friends. All they have to sell is what comes out of their mouths. What would happen if they all started blabbing for nothing? You're not giving him any free publicity, you know. Ah, you mean that you've heard of lawyers who help people without getting any money or recognition for it? Never happens. They get money or publicity. They don't give it away. There's nothing in it for the lawyers. Their whole world would crumble. Goodbye Hawaii. Goodbye sports car. Forget your life, Billy's busy with his own.

Or here's the other possibility. Billy, your life-long friend, talks and talks and talks. He knows all about your case, right off the bat. He predicts the worst. He shakes his head a lot. You're gonna lose everything, man. You're never gonna get a divorce. You're going down the big drain of ruination along with all the other wife dumpers in the world. I see guys like you in court all the time. Destroyed. I'm just going to have to sit here and watch it happen, I guess. Hmmmm. You have some questions? Let's hear 'em. Well, your lawyer sucks. You better get another one. Sorry, I don't know anyone I can recommend off hand. Oh, the judge said that? Yeah, you'll lose your house, never see your kids, probably land in jail, and end up bankrupt just as your beautiful girlfriend is walking out on you …

What a friend! But you're alone and vulnerable.

You say, What should I do?

Billy laughs. Nothing, man. You're finished, as far as I can see it. Then he goes off to bilk some other poor sucker with a case just like yours.

So much for lawyer friends. Oxymorons.

On the other hand, women will call you. Single women. They'll hear your big news and want to give you some Southern comfort. They'll want to be your friend, even if they happen to be friends with your wife. Hey, I know you. You're my wife's friend from the office, aren't you? That's right, she's the one you met, the one your wife used to talk about. She's just trying to help. Need a nice home-cooked meal? Some sex? A new wife? She'll be right over.

You'll probably get calls from the single women who hung around year after year, waiting to be fixed up with your unmarried friends. Remember this one? You and your wife tried to fix her up a few times, just to be nice. Now she's calling you and she's about as sexy as a cement truck. Thanks, but no thanks.

There will probably be one or two friends, male or female, who really are on your side. They can't help much, but they'll hang out with you. They won't report back to your wife. They'll care about you and do whatever they can to help out. They'll give you moral support which is all you really want from your friends anyway, isn't it? If you're lucky, one or two of them will stand by you when the going gets grim.

Other than these few friends, you're out in the cold. Count on starting over. But, hey, you wanted freedom and there are billions of people in the world. You can make new friends. You can meet women. You can pick your friends without having to satisfy your wife's tastes, which might not have always been the same as your own. You might be surprised by how many new people find you attractive and interesting. There's nothing like an unattached male monkey swinging through the trees to make the lady apes sit up and take notice.

While you're out working on you're new life there will be one thing about your old friends that will probably bother you. It's called the "missionary problem." See, your wife is keeping busy, too. She's enlisting people, sending missionaries to you to gather information, to pressure you into going back, and to make you feel guilty and miserable. It's one thing to hang up on Wife Two, but it's another to cope with an old friend or a client who is giving you the so-concerned speech over lunch or a drink. You can think to yourself, "Kiss off, weasel." But you do have to sit there and take it. The poor kids. The poor wife. She's so depressed. She calls me three times a week. They're hoping you'll come home … You've heard it all before by now.

Eventually, you'll get good at sniffing out the missionaries and refusing to eat with them. How are you supposed to eat when your former friend is spewing this kind of verbal pollution into your face? Of course, you care, my friend. I'll be sure to remember this wonderful lunch always. Goodbye (forever).

As long as you know in advance that you are basically alone in this world, you won't be too disappointed when people who once meant something to you suddenly stab you in the back. Not too disappointed. Sure, it hurts. But you'll find out who your real friends are, even if there are only a couple of them. The bottom line is, don't expect anything from your friends, all right? Don't expect cash loans, favors, advice, or help of any kind. Whatever you get from your friends, if anything, is pure gravy.

So it's time to suck it up, and you can start by changing out the soundtrack playing in your head. Rip out the *We Are The World* and *Let's Stay Together* and throw them in the trash. Start playing *Freebird, Big Pimpin'* and *Sexual Healing* on maximum rotation until they sink in. Heck, unbox the stereo and crank up your favorite CDs as loud as you want, as many times as you want. It's your place, you can do that if you want to.

Your best friend is you now. It's your girlfriend or the new women you meet. It's your work, your future, and your own clear head. That's friendship, true blue.

Chapter Twelve

Young Women All Over You

You might think, after reading this book, that I don't like women (despite being one myself). This is not true. I love women. I just don't like greedy, self-serving, conniving women. Men can be that way too, and when they are, I don't like them either. It's very simple. A person is a person, man or woman.

If you've had a horrible marriage and a few affairs that were bummers, don't give up. The woman of your dreams is out there. So what if you accidently married the wrong one? There's still time to find the real thing. And with the right attitude – by that I mean light-hearted and easygoing – you can enjoy looking for her, too.

There are hundreds of books around that will tell you how to have sex without catching AIDS and how to cope with bodily fluids. You don't need this book for that. Get yourself up-to-date. Learn the rules. And then get going with the girls!

Let's face it, buddy, you're not fresh out of college. You've been here before. Maybe you have a few kids, you've bought a house or an apartment, you've found out what you want to do with your career. You're not a green thing anymore. And this actually makes you more attractive.

If you have a girlfriend, she already appreciates you and what you've been through. Make sure she knows that you did it for yourself – not just for her. For godssakes, don't lay a guilt trip on her about tearing you away from your kids and your easy life. If you did it only for her and not for yourself, you'd never be able to get through it. Still, there will be hard times ahead. Your relationship will either get so strong and close that you practically become the same person, or it will fall apart under the strain of the divorce.

Take a moment and consider the position of your girlfriend. She's thrown herself into this out of love. Maybe she underestimated the difficulty, expense, and trouble ahead for you. Surely, she underestimated it for herself. Once a normal, single, carefree woman, she is now the ultimate whore. The homebreaker, the heathen she-devil with her seething sexuality, tearing the loving husband out of the arms of his noble wife. It's part of the pop culture – fatal attraction.

Try to imagine what she must be going through. Vulnerable to lawsuits and hate mail and raging social condemnation, your girlfriend needs your support as much as you need hers. Don't leave her out in the cold, okay? She's your future, your oasis, the woman of your dreams, and she needs you, too.

Give her all the affection and love you've been holding back all these years, and you'll keep each other together through the tough times. If the relationship is not the real thing, you'll find out soon enough. But don't let your angry wife come between you! She'd love to see you break up because of the trouble she causes. Stand strong together, you and the woman you love, against all the fury and rage of your soon-to-be ex.

There aren't more than a handful of things that I believe in, but one of them is that two people who love each other should be together. I predict that, in the next century, this shackle called marriage and this medieval punishment called divorce will fall to pieces. People will get sick and tired of the hypocrites on TV telling them how to live their lives. Family Values don't need to be crammed down your throat if you love your wife. And sex isn't really a death-defying act of social terrorism the way the goody-goodies make it out to be. Yes, I predict sometime in this twenty-first century, society will abandon its compulsion to condemn men to marriage prison for life.

We're stuck, though, in the here and now. You can't escape from the lawyers anymore than you can escape from the social climate that claims your generation.

So we deal with it.

Now for the fun part. If you don't have a girlfriend right now, maybe you don't really want one yet. Or maybe you haven't found the perfect one for you. In the meantime, you just want to relax and go out with a few women and take a break from the pressure. It's one thing to make a lifelong commitment complete with kids and life insurance, and it's another to go out to dinner and a movie. Or just hang out at your favorite bar, enjoy your drink, and look around. No rush. You've got the rest of your life to yourself.

Have you noticed that everyone thinks that men enjoy going out with young women just because they're young? That's stupid! Young women can be terrific or disgusting, just like older women. Sure, there are more young women available because they're not married yet. That's math. But if you pick a younger woman, you pick her for a lot of reasons, not just her birthdate. Don't let the hysterical masses of aging women, their biological alarm clocks ringing out of control, control you. You don't have an obligation to rescue anyone from mommy-mania. You have your own agenda. If you want to date a twenty-one year old woman who hasn't even thought yet about marriage and children, that's your choice. A woman is a woman, and she doesn't have to be over thirty-five to be interesting or sensual or intelligent.

You choose. Would you like to explore the world of forty and up? If you're coming off one of those bouncy co-eds in Reeboks, you might be drawn to someone a bit more sophisticated. Yeah, that'd be nice. A woman who wears high heels and lipstick and knows how to eat with a knife and fork. Neat.

Maybe you'll go for a married woman who just wants sex, sex, sex. After a bad marriage, it might be just the thing to pick you up.

Or some casual dating might be nice. A few trips to local parks, beaches, or other places where a beautiful woman might relax on a Sunday afternoon. If you don't like bars, no problem. There's more than one way to catch a cat.

Beware of one thing, though. Your new social life will spark uncontrollable rage in your married male friends and colleagues. They'll be cynical and critical and insanely jealous. They will rant and rave about their wonderful wives until you could lose your lunch. They'll want to know every single thing about every single woman you date. They'd like to pass judgment. And they'd like you to know that they, personally, disapprove of your bad behavior. For sure, they're going to resurrect the old mid-life-crisis psychobabble from the Seventies. Well, sit back and enjoy it.

Obviously, wild horses couldn't drag you into bed with the dried fruit they're married to and they know it. They're stuck. Their lives are over. The guys who badger you the most will be the ones with the worst wives. You know their wives. You've been to those dinner parties and seen those terrified, unloved women digging their nails into their lumpy husbands. Now you represent everything those guys wish for but will never have. They're limping along in some little affair that will never lead anywhere, or they're loyal to their wives out of fear and ideology. They'll do whatever they can to spoil your party, so don't let your guard down or they'll grab their chance to make you pay. Jealousy is a powerful force of nature.

And, speaking of danger, you better watch out for any inclinations to indulge in the following list of things and don't let yourself do them:

- Don't date your wife's friends, unless you're really in love with one of them.
- Don't date women from your office, unless you're really in love with one of them.
- Don't date your lawyer.
- Don't go to your old hangouts with your new women.
- Don't bring your dates home when your kids are spending the night.
- Don't introduce your kids to your casual dates.

- Don't talk about your divorce with your casual dates.

Don't, don't, don't. What a drag!

What about the bright side? What about young women all over you? What about being alive for the first time in years? Finally feeling like yourself again? What about it, man? Celebrate! Live it up! Take the pleasure with the pain. You've earned it.

Okay, your wife is not going to simply disappear or spontaneously combust, but she won't be with you on Friday night when you meet Jennifer or Rachel or Heather. She won't be hanging on you when you discover that curvy, sexy Kristy has a brilliant mind and a great heart. Wow, Kristy understands me. She gets it. She's the real thing!

Or imagine the ultimate dinner date. Your wife is *not* sitting there at the table with you in stony silence. Instead, you're chatting intimately with Amber. Her beautiful lips move as she chews her little bites of salad. Her soft, long hair swings as she walks to the dance floor on your arm.

The rewards for having courage and acting on your convictions are rich. The beauty of taking control of your life, correcting a big mistake, and making way for some kind of real love in your future will hold you up when the blows come pounding down on your head.

Your wife, whether she's a One, a Two, or a Three, will want nothing less than your total destruction. She will devote herself to ruining you. She will torture you with your own children. She will seek to infect you with guilt. She, who knows your every weakness, will twist the trust you had in the past by forcing you onto an excruciating legal rack.

As a father, you will suffer. Financially, you will suffer. As a professional whatever-you-are, you will suffer. But as a man, as an individual, as a human being with a right to live, and have love in your life, you will triumph.

APPENDIX

Charts Current
As Of November 2004

Adapted from *Family Law in the 50 States*, published by the Family Law Section of the American Bar Association. Copyright © 2004–2005 American Bar Association. Reprinted by permission. Please seek legal counsel to ensure accuracy of the information provided. Additional advice is available at:

www.divorceassetprotection.com

Chart 1: Alimony/Spousal Support Factors

STATE	Statutory List*	Marital Fault Not Considered	Marital Fault Relevant	Standard of Living	Status as Parent Considered
Alabama			x	x	
Alaska	x	x		x	x
Arizona	x	x		x	x
Arkansas		x			
California	x		x	x	
Colorado	x	x		x	x
Connecticut	x		x	x	x
Delaware	x	x		x	x
Dist. of Columbia		x	x		
Florida	x		x	x	
Georgia	x		x	x	
Hawaii	x	x		x	x
Idaho	x		x		
Illinois	x	x		x	x
Indiana	x	x			
Iowa	x	x		x	x
Kansas		x			
Kentucky	x		x^1	x	
Louisiana	x		x		x
Maine	x	x			
Maryland	x		x	x	
Massachusetts	x		x	x	
Michigan	x		x		
Minnesota	x	x		x	x
Mississippi			x		
Missouri	x		x	x	x
Montana	x	x		x	x
Nebraska	x	x		x	x
Nevada		x		x	x
New Hampshire	x		x	x	x
New Jersey	x		x	x	x
New Mexico	x	x		x	
New York	x		x	x	x
North Carolina	x		x	x	
North Dakota			x	x	
Ohio	x	x		x	x
Oklahoma		x		x	x
Oregon	x	x		x	x
Pennsylvania	x		x	x	
Rhode Island	x		x	x	x
South Carolina	x		x	x	x
South Dakota			x	x	
Tennessee	x		x	x	x
Texas	x		x	x	x
Utah	x		x	x	x
Vermont	x	x		x	x
Virginia	x		x	x	
Washington	x	x		x	
West Virginia	x		x		x
Wisconsin	x	x		x	x
Wyoming			x		

* Although there is a statutory list of factors, the judge may in its discretion consider other factors under the particular circumstances of the case.
1. Only fault on the part of the party seeking alimony.

From *Family Law in the 50 States,* published by the Family Law Section of the American Bar Association Copyright © 2004-2005 American Bar Association. Reprinted by permission.

Chart 2: Custody Criteria

STATE	Statutory Guidelines	Children's Wishes	Joint Custody*	Cooperative Parent	Domestic Violence	Health	Attorney or GAL
Alabama	x	x	x		x		
Alaska	x	x	x		x		x
Arizona	x	x	x	x	x	x	x
Arkansas					x		
California	x	x		x	x	x	x
Colorado	x	x	x^1	x	x	x	x
Connecticut		x	x				x
Delaware	x	x	x		x	x	x
Dist. of Columbia	x	x	x	x	x	x	x
Florida	x	x	x	x	x	x	x
Georgia	x	x	x		x		x
Hawaii	x^2	x^8	x^7		x		x^9
Idaho	x	x	x		x	x	
Illinois	x	x	x	x	x	x	x
Indiana	x	x	x	x	x	x	x
Iowa	x	x	x	x	x	x	x
Kansas	x	x	x	x	x	x	
Kentucky	x	x	x	x	x	x	x
Louisiana	x	x	x		x		
Maine	x	x	x		x		x
Maryland		x	x	x	x	x	x
Massachusetts			x		x		x
Michigan	x	x	x	x	x	x	x
Minnesota	x	x	x		x	x	x
Mississippi	x		x			x	x^2
Missouri	x	x	x	x	x	x	x
Montana	x	x	x		x		x
Nebraska	x	x	x		x	x	x
Nevada	x	x	x	x	x		x
New Hampshire	x	x	x		x		x
New Jersey	x	x	x	x	x	x	x
New Mexico	x	x	x	x	x	x	x
New York		x			x^2		x
North Carolina		x^2	x		x	x	
North Dakota	x	x	x	x^3	x	x	
Ohio	x^2	x	x^{10}		x	x	x
Oklahoma	x	x	x	x	x		x^4
Oregon	x	x	x	x	x		x^3
Pennsylvania	x	x	x	x	x	x	x
Rhode Island		x	x	x	x	x	x
South Carolina		x	x	x	x	x	x
South Dakota		x	x	x	x		
Tennessee	x	x^5	x^6	x	x		x
Texas	x	x	x	x	x	x	x
Utah	x	x	x	x			x
Vermont	x		x		x		x
Virginia	x	x^2	x	x	x	x	x^4
Washington	x	x			x	x	x
West Virginia	x	x	x		x		
Wisconsin	x	x	x	x	x	x	x
Wyoming	x	x	x	x	x	x	

* Court in the exercise of its sound discretion shall consider the best interests and welfare of the minor child.
** At least joint legal custody.
1. Now uses term "parental rights and responsibilities."
2. Considered if child is old enough.
3. By case law.
4. Not mandatory.
5. The court must listen to the reasonable preferences of a child twelve or older, giving greater weight to the preferences of older children. The court may at its discretion hear the reasonable preference of children under the age of twelve.
6. In divorce, the courts no longer use "custody" terminology, instead, separately allocating between the parents (1) residential time; and, (2) parental responsibility in specific areas such as non-emergency health care, religion, education and extra-curricular activities.
7. Emphasizes "best interest of child."
8. If child is of sufficient age and capacity to reason, and form intelligent preference.
9. Appointment of custody evaluators and guardians ad litem authorized by administrative rule.
10. Now uses the term "shared parenting."

Chart 3: Child Support Guidelines

STATE	Income Share	Percent of Income	Extraordinary Medical Deduction	Child-care Deduction	College Support	Shared Parenting Time Offset
Alabama	x	x	x ^{p}	x ^{m}	x	
Alaska		x	x ^{m}	x	x	x
Arizona	x		x ^{m}	x ^{p}		
Arkansas		x	x ^{d}	x ^{d}		
California	x		x ^{m}	x ^{m}		x
Colorado	x		x ^{m}	x ^{m}		x
Connecticut	x		x ^{d}		x	
Delaware			x ^{m}	x ^{m}		x*
Dist. of Columbia		x	x ^{d}	x	x	x
Florida	x		x ^{p}	x ^{m}		
Georgia		x	x ^{p}	x ^{m}		
Hawaii	x	x	x ^{m3}	x	x	x
Idaho	x		x ^{m}	x ^{p}		x
Illinois		x			x	
Indiana	x		x ^{p}	x ^{m}	x	x ^{4}
Iowa	x			x ^{m}	x	x
Kansas	x			x ^{m}		x
Kentucky	x		x ^{m}	x ^{p}		
Louisiana	x		x ^{m}	x ^{m}		
Maine	x		x ^{m}	x ^{m}		
Maryland	x		x ^{m}	x ^{m}		
Massachusetts		x	x ^{m}	x	x	
Michigan	x		x ^{m}	x ^{m}	x	x
Minnesota		x		x ^{m}		x
Mississippi		x	x ^{d}	x ^{d}		
Missouri	x		x	x	x	x
Montana			x ^{m}	x ^{m}		
Nebraska	x		x ^{d}	x ^{m}		x
Nevada		x	x ^{m}	x ^{d}		x
New Hampshire		x	x ^{d}		x	
New Jersey	x		x ^{m}	x ^{m}	x	x
New Mexico	x		x ^{p}	x ^{m}		x
New York	x		x ^{m}	x ^{m}	x	
North Carolina	x		x ^{p}	x ^{m}		x
North Dakota		x	x ^{d}			
Ohio	x		x ^{p}	x ^{m}	x ^{p}	
Oklahoma	x		x ^{a}	x ^{m}		x
Oregon	x		x ^{p}	x ^{m}	x	x
Pennsylvania	x		x $^{m/d}$	x ^{m}		
Rhode Island	x		x ^{d}	x ^{m}		
South Carolina	x		x ^{d}	x ^{m}	x	
South Dakota	x		x ^{d}	x ^{d}		
Tennessee		x	x ^{m}		x ^{1}	x ^{2}
Texas		x	x ^{m}	x ^{d}		
Utah	x		x ^{m}	x $^{m/p}$		x
Vermont	x		x ^{m}	x ^{m}		x
Virginia	x		x ^{a}	x ^{a}		x
Washington	x		x ^{m}	x ^{m}	x	
West Virginia	x		x ^{m}	x ^{m}		x
Wisconsin		x	x ^{m}	x ^{d}		
Wyoming	x		x ^{d}	x ^{d}		x

* by case law
a mandatory add-ons
m mandatory deduction
p permissive deduction
d deviation factor
1. May be voluntarily agreed by the parties, in which case it is contractually enforceable thereafter, but otherwise may not be imposed by the court. However, an obligor parent may be required to con-tribute during a child's minority to an educational trust fund which would be used for college costs post-minority.
2. Support may be increased or decreased it the obligor spends more or less than 80 days (the putative normal amount of time) with a child.
3. Credit given for actual cost of health care insurance premium paid for children.
4. Starting January 1, 2004

Chart 4: Grounds for Divorce and Residency Requirements

STATE	No Fault Sole Ground	No Fault Added to Traditional	Incompatibility	Living Separate and Apart	Judicial Separation Requirements	Durational
Alabama		x	x	2 years	x	6 months
Alaska	x		x	2 years	x	6 months
Arizona	x	x[1]			x	90 days
Arkansas		x		18 mos.	x	60 days
California	x				x	6 months*
Colorado	x				x	90 days
Connecticut		x		18 mos.	x	1 year
Delaware		x	x	6 mos.		6 months
Dist. of Columbia	x			1 year	x	6 months
Florida	x					6 months
Georgia		x				6 months
Hawaii				2 years[3]	x	6 months[4]
Idaho		x			x	6 weeks
Illinois		x		2 years	x	90 days
Indiana			x	x		60 days
Iowa	x				x	1 year
Kansas			x		x	60 days
Kentucky	x			60 days	x	180 days
Louisiana		x1		6 months[2]	x	6 months
Maine		x			x	6 months
Maryland		x		1 year	x	1 year
Massachusetts		x			x	None
Michigan	x				x	6 months
Minnesota	x				x	180 days
Mississippi		x				6 months
Missouri		x		1–2 years	x	90 days
Montana	x		x	180 days	x	90 days
Nebraska	x				x	1 year
Nevada			x	1 year	x	6 weeks
New Hampshire		x		2 years		1 year
New Jersey		x		18 mos.		1 year
New Mexico		x	x		x	6 months
New York		x		1 year	x	1 year
North Carolina		x		1 year	x	6 months
North Dakota		x			x	6 months
Ohio		x	x	1 year		6 months
Oklahoma				x	x	6 months
Oregon	x				x	6 months
Pennsylvania		x		2 years		6 months
Rhode Island		x		3 years	x	1 year
South Carolina		x		1 year	x	3 months (both residents)
South Dakota		x			x	None
Tennessee		x		2 years	x	6 months
Texas		x		3 years		6 months
Utah		x		3 years	x	90 days
Vermont		x		6 months		6 months
Virginia		x		1 year	x	6 months
Washington	x					1 year
West Virginia		x		1 year	x	1 year
Wisconsin	x				x	6 months
Wyoming		x	x	x		60 days

* California requires domicile as distinguished from residency for jurisdictional purposes.
1. Covenant marriage statutes establish specific grounds for divorce for covenant marriages.
2. Two years for covenant marriages.
3. Grounds are either marriage irretrievably broken or two years separation.
4. Six months in state and three months in circuit waiting for divorce itself, but can file as soon as residency established.

Chart 5: Property Division

STATE	Community Property	Only Marital Divided	Statutory List of Factors	Nonmonetary Contributions	Economic Misconduct	Contribution to Education
Alabama		x		x		x
Alaska	x[1]		x	x	x	
Arizona	x				x	x
Arkansas		x	x	x		
California	x		x	x	x	x
Colorado		x	x	x	x	
Connecticut			x	x	x	x
Delaware		x	x	x	x	x
Dist. of Columbia		x	x	x	x	
Florida		x	x	x	x	x
Georgia		x				
Hawaii		x[4]	x[5]	x[2]	x[3]	
Idaho	x		x			
Illinois		x	x	x	x	
Indiana		x	x	x	x	x
Iowa			x	x	x	x
Kansas			x		x	
Kentucky		x	x	x	x	x
Louisiana	x					
Maine		x	x	x	x	
Maryland		x	x	x	x	
Massachusetts			x	x	x	x
Michigan		x		x	x	x
Minnesota		x	x	x	x	
Mississippi		x	x	x	x	x
Missouri		x	x	x	x	x
Montana			x	x	x	
Nebraska		x		x		
Nevada	x	x		x	x	x
New Hampshire			x	x	x	x
New Jersey		x	x	x	x	x
New Mexico	x					
New York		x	x	x	x	x
North Carolina		x	x	x	x	x
North Dakota				x	x	x
Ohio		x	x	x	x	x
Oklahoma		x		x	x	
Oregon				x	x	x
Pennsylvania		x	x	x	x	x
Rhode Island		x	x	x	x	x
South Carolina		x	x	x	x	x
South Dakota				x	x	
Tennessee		x	x	x	x	x
Texas	x				x	
Utah						
Vermont			x	x	x	x
Virginia		x	x	x	x	x
Washington	x		x			
West Virginia		x	x	x	x	x
Wisconsin	x	x	x	x	x	x
Wyoming		x	x	x		

1. The parties by contract can agree to make some or all of their marital property community property.
2. During marriage nonmonetary contributions do not affect property division nor does the lack of them.
3. No statutory provision apply; case law is mixed.
4. During marriage nonmonetary contributions do not affect property division, nor does the lack of them.
5. No statutory provisions; case law is mixed.

Chart 6: Third Party Visitation

STATE	Stepparents	Grandparents Death of their Child	Grandparents Child Divorce	Out of Wedlock	Any Interested Party
Alabama			x	x	
Alaska	x	x	x	x	
Arizona	x[1]	x	x	x	
Arkansas		x	x		
California	x	x	x		
Colorado		x	x	x	
Connecticut	x	x	x	x	
Delaware	x		x		
District of Columbia					
Florida		x	x	x	
Georgia		x	x		
Hawaii	x		x		
Idaho			x	x	
Illinois		x		x	
Indiana	x	x	x	x	
Iowa					
Kansas	x	x	x	x	
Kentucky		x	x	x	
Louisiana		x	x		
Maine	x	x	x	x	
Maryland		x	x		
Massachusetts		x	x		
Michigan	x	x	x		
Minnesota	x	x	x	x	
Mississippi		x	x		
Missouri		x	x	x	
Montana		x	x	x	
Nebraska	x	x	x		
Nevada		x	x	x	
New Hampshire	x	x	x	x	
New Jersey	x	x	x	x	
New Mexico	x	x	x	x	
New York	x	x	x	x	
North Carolina			x		
North Dakota	x	x	x		
Ohio	x	x	x	x	x[2]
Oklahoma		x	x	x	
Oregon	x	x	x	x	
Pennsylvania		x	x		
Rhode Island		x	x		
South Carolina		x	x	x	
South Dakota		x	x	x	
Tennessee	x		x		
Texas	x	x	x	x	
Utah	x	x	x	x	
Vermont		x	x		
Virginia					x[3]
Washington	x		x		
West Virginia		x	x	x	
Wisconsin		x	x		
Wyoming	x	x	x		x

1. New *in loco parentis* bill allows visitation and in rare cases custody to these in loco parents.
2. Extends only to relatives of minor child.
3. This includes any relative or a stepparent.
4. Only if stepparent is established as child's "psychological parent" under case law.

- 134 -

Chart 7: Appointment Laws in Adoption, Guardianship, Unmarried Parent and Divorce Cases*

STATE	Adoption	Guardianship	Unmarried	Parent Divorce
Alabama	Req'd if contested	Req'd if contested	Req'd if minor is a party	GAL – Discretionary - Att'y
Alaska	No statute	No statute	No statute	GAL or Att'y - Discretionary - Att'y/Gov't Att'y
Arizona	No statute	No statute	No statute	Att'y or GAL - Discretionary - GAL - Professional
Arkansas	Discretionary	Discretionary	No statute	Att'y - Discretionary
California	Discretionary	Discretionary	Req'd if minor is a party	Hybrid - Discretionary - Att'y/Gov't Att'y
Colorado	Discretionary	Discretionary	Discretionary	Att'y or GAL - Discretionary - GAL - Att'y/Other Prof.
Connecticut	Discretionary	Discretionary	Req'd if minor is a party	Att'y or GAL - Discretionary -GAL - Att'y/Other Prof.
Delaware	Discretionary	Discretionary	Discretionary	Att'y or GAL - Discretionary -GAL - Att'y/Other Prof.
Dist. of Columbia	No statute	No statute	No statute	GAL - Discretionary - Att'y
Florida	Discretionary	Discretionary	Discretionary	Att'y or GAL req'd if abuse involved - GAL Att'y/Certified
Georgia	Discretionary	Discretionary	Discretionary	GAL - Discretionary - varies by county
Hawaii	Discretionary	Discretionary	Req'd if minor is a party	GAL - Discretionary - Att'y/ Gov't/Att'y/ Professional
Idaho	No statute	No statute	No statute	Att'y - Discretionary
Illinois	Required	Discretionary	Discretionary	Att'y - Hybrid or GAL -Discretionary Att'y/ Gov't/Att'y
Indiana	Req'd if contested	Discretionary	Req'd if minor is a party	GAL - Discretionary - Att'y/CASA trained
Iowa	Discretionary	Discretionary	Discretionary	Att'y or GAL - Discretionary - Att'y
Kansas	Discretionary	Discretionary	Req'd if minor is a party	GAL - Discretionary - Att'y/Other Professional
Kentucky	Req'd if contested	Discretionary	Req'd if minor is a party	GAL - Discretionary - Att'y
Louisiana	Discretionary	Discretionary	No statute	Att'y - Req'd if abuse involved
Maine	Discretionary	Discretionary	No statute	GAL - Discretionary - Att'y/Other Professional
Maryland	Req'd if minor over 10	Req'd if minor over 10	Required	Att'y or GAL - Discretionary - Att'y
Massachusetts	Required	Required	Discretionary	Att'y or GAL - Discretionary - GAL - Att'y/disinterested
Michigan	Discretionary	Discretionary	Discretionary	Hybrid - Discretionary - Att'y
Minnesota	Discretionary	Discretionary	Discretionary	GAL - Req'd if abuse involved - Att'y/Professional
Mississippi	Discretionary	Discretionary	Discretionary	GAL - Req'd if abuse involved - Att'y/Professional
Missouri	Required	Discretionary	Required	GAL - Req'd if abuse - Att'y
Montana	Discretionary	Discretionary	Required	GAL - Discretionary - Att'y/Other
Nebraska	Required	Required	Required	Att'y or GAL - Discretionary - Att'y
Nevada	No statute	Discretionary	Required	GAL - Discretionary - Att'y/Other Professional
New Hampshire	Discretionary	Discretionary	Discretionary	GAL - Discretionary - Att'y/Other Professional
New Jersey	Discretionary	Discretionary	Discretionary	Att'y or GAL - Discretionary - GAL - Att'y/Other Prof.
New Mexico	Req'd if contested	Required	Req'd if minor is a party	GAL - Discretionary - Att'y
New York	Required	Required	Required	Att'y - Discretionary - Att'y/Gov't Att y
North Carolina	Discretionary	Discretionary	Required	GAL - Discretionary - Att'y
North Dakota	Required	Discretionary	Required	GAL - Discretionary - Att'y
Ohio	Discretionary	Discretionary	Requires party's request	Att'y or GAL - Discretionary - GAL - Att'y/Other Prof.
Oklahoma	Req'd if contested	Req'd if contested	No statute	GAL - Discretionary - Att'y
Oregon	No statute	Discretionary	No statute	Att'y - Req'd if a minor requests
Pennsylvania	Required	Required	No statute	Att'y or Hybrid - Discretionary - Att'y
Rhode Island	Discretionary	Discretionary	Discretionary	Att'y or GAL - Discretionary - Does not specify
South Carolina	Required	Discretionary	Req'd if action seeks to legitimize minor	GAL - Discretionary - Att'y/Other
South Dakota	No statute	Discretionary	No statute	Att'y - Discretionary
Tennessee	Discretionary	Discretionary	Discretionary	Att'y or GAL - Discretionary - Does not specify
Texas	Discretionary	Discretionary	Discretionary	Att'y or GAL - Req'd if in best interest - GAL - Att'y/Adult
Utah	Discretionary	Discretionary	Req'd if minor is a party	Att'y or GAL -Discretionary -GAL - Att'y/Gov't Att'y
Vermont	Req'd if contested	Discretionary	Req'd if minor is a party	Att'y - Req'd if a minor
Virginia	Discretionary	Discretionary	Req'd if minor is a party	Att'y or GAL - Req'd if abuse involved - GAL - Att'y
Washington	Discretionary	Discretionary	Discretionary	GAL - Discretionary - Att'y/Other
West Virginia	Discretionary	Discretionary	Req'd if father brings action	GAL - Req'd if abuse involved - GAL does not specify
Wisconsin	Req'd if contested	Discretionary	Required	GAL - Req'd if contested - Att'y
Wyoming	Discretionary	Discretionary	Req'd if minor is a party	Req'd if abuse involved

* Prepared by Linda Rio, Director of the ABA Child Custody Project.

INDEX

lawyers and, 54
types of wives and, 16-17, 52-54, 76-80
begging and pleading by, 101-102
bribing wife and, 77
Child support, 6, 37, 61-62, 96
Children, 2, 13, 50, 52-53, 55, 59-62, 88, 104-107, 112-113
communication with, 59
friends and, 112
girlfriend and, 55
going back to, 104
guilt and, 23-24
kidnapping, 61
living with, 55-56. *See also* Child custody
money to, 36-37. *See also* Child support
reaction to divorce by, 51-52
wife's manipulation of, 51-62, 101-103, 106-109
Communication
with children, 59-60
with girlfriend, 33
papers for, 77-78
public opinion about, 61
preparation for, 89
Cook Islands, 44
Cooperation, appearance of, 97
Counseling, 23, 104
Couples therapy, 104
Court, 3, 46, 90, 114. *See also* Judges; Lawyers
bias of, towards wife, 37, 62, 90, 93
girlfriend and, 61

orders of, 66, 96
representing yourself in, 91
Credit cards, 20, 83, 98
private investigators and, 98
Credit unions, 41
Credit line accounts, 83
Custody. *See also* Child custody
Databases, 19, 39, 98
Dating, 98, 101-102, 104, 122
rules of, 123-124
Death, faking, 33, 45
Detectives. *See also* Private investigators
Divorce
bankruptcy and, 96
bribing wife and, 77
children, telling about, 59
children as weapons in, 51-62
children's reactions to, 51-52
as civil case, 46, 94-95
cost of, 6, 33, 62
devastation of, 46
in different states, 10, 37
in future, 6, 121
grounds for, 29, 67
no-fault, 68, 78
wife, telling about, 76-82
ERISA, 18
Family. *See also* Children; Wife
Family Values, 1-7, 25-26, 121
Federal Bureau of Investigation (FBI), 41
FedEx, 107
Feminists, 4-5, 17, 57
Foreign countries. *See also* specific countries
Foreign-immigration lawyers, 78
Friends, 2-3, 12-13, 15-17, 23,

privacy, 68-69
Lawyers, 20, 87-95
  being your own, 91
  bias of, towards wife, 93
  child custody and, 57
  child support and, 61
  choosing, 89-92
  fees of, 67, 92, 94, 101
  foreign-immigration, 78
  friends as, 91,114-115
  image of, 87-88, 90-91
  inexpensive, 77-78, 94
  judges and, 96-97
  public opinion and, 61
Leases, 29, 31. *See also* Apartment
Letters, 83, 101, 107-109. *See also* Mail
Liechtenstein, 44
Love, 49-51, 53-54, 60-62, 71, 77, 81-82, 93, 98, 103, 109, 120-125
  girlfriend and, 11, 13, 27
  guilt and, 22
  secrecy and, 81
Luxembourg, 43-44
Lying, 59
Mail, 30, 32, 40-41, 43, 108, 120
  harassment by, 107-108
Mailbox services, 41, 68
Maintenance, court-ordered versus voluntary, 88
Malaysia, 44
Marriage. *See also* Wife
  distractions from, 27
  going back to, 102-104
  reasons for, 10-11
  divorce and, 65-66
  without girlfriends, 27

Money, 35-45, 61-62, 72. *See also* Business; Career; Divorce, cost of; Net worth; Child support
  girlfriend and, 29
  hiding, 38-46
  moving around, 41
  secrecy and, 28, 38-46
  specific assets to children, 36-37.
Mortgage, 18, 69
Mother, wife as unfit, 56
Moving away, 28-33
  alone, 30-32
  business and, 72
  girlfriend, with, 29-30
  out of state, 72, 89-90
  personal papers and researching, 67-70
  telling wife and, 81-82
Net worth, 65, 97
No-fault divorce laws, 68, 78
Overdrafts, 83
Paper trail, 40-42. *See also* Databases
Papers, divorce, 78
Paralegals, 67
Paranoia, 15, 18, 112
Partners, business, 71
Passport, 43, 97
Paycheck, 70
Pension plans, 18
Phone. *See also* Telephone
Possessions, 65
  bribing wife and, 77
Prison, 42, 46, 62, 97, 121
Privacy, 20, 44, 71, 76. *See also* Secrecy
  banking and, 44

ABOUT THE ARTIST

Scott Reed, Cover Design and Illustrations

After graduating from the Art Institute of Pittsburgh, Scott Reed began a career in graphic design and commercial art, producing illustrations and designs for Disney, Wal-Mart, Marvel Comics, United Way, Target, Remax, Home Depot and Paramount Pictures. Scott brings 15 years of graphic design experience to his full-service studio. Combining traditional illustration with cutting-edge computer graphics and web development, Scott provides unique, creative solutions to a wide variety of businesses. An award-winning cartoonist and designer and one of the pioneers of digital comics on the web, Scott's prolific and versatile work has been described as "old school" with a contemporary flair, and praised by USA Today and SciFi Channel as "stylish" and "cool."

www.websbestdesigns.com
www.websbestcomics.com

ABOUT THE MUSIC

Splitsville

The Audio CD version of *How to Dump Your Wife* features music from *Incorporated*, the new album from Splitsville. With shades of Coldplay, Weezer, Elvis Costello and the Beach Boys, the Splitsville sound has garnered legions of fans worldwide and passionate critical acclaim. Their music is now available at www.itunes.com.

> "In today's sea of musical mediocrity floats at least one buoy of hope: Splitsville."   — *Amplifier Magazine*

Visit
www.splitsville.com

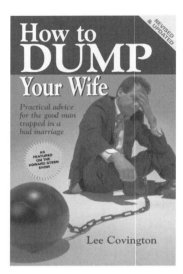

GOT A BRUTAL DIVORCE STORY – OR SOME GREAT ADVICE FOR YOUR FELLOW MAN?

For God's sake, please send it to us! Email your tale of woe or brilliant divorce strategy to **publisher@kickassmedia.com** and include your name (unless you prefer to be anonymous). Any submission makes you eligible for the *"How to Dump Your Wife*™ Raffle"* with great prizes to help you as you re-enter the world of the living (go to **www.menstactics.com** for more details). Selected entries will also receive special mention in the next edition of *How to Dump Your Wife.* Send in your tips today!

(All entries become property of KickAssMedia.)

To collect your FREE gift worth $75.00
send an email to **gift@howtodumpyourwife.com**

DON'T GAMBLE WITH YOUR ASSETS

Lawsuits? Divorce? Marriage? Running a business? Own real estate? Everyone needs a basic asset protection plan. For the finest in asset protection services, visit:

www.divorceassetprotection.com
or
www.assetprotectiongenius.com

JOIN THE "MEN'S TACTICS" COMMUNITY

Please visit **www.menstactics.com** to view our entire selection of indispensable products for the savvy man. You'll also find great advice on life, love, sex, divorce, travel, asset protection, and much, much more.

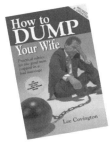

ORDER A BOOK TODAY
FOR A GOOD MAN TRAPPED
IN A BAD MARRIAGE
(Bulk Discounts Available)

To order please visit **www.kickassmedia.com**
or Call us toll-free at 1-877-MY COOL BOOK
or Fax the order form below to: 1-877-692-7441
or Mail the order form to the address below:
KickAssMedia, 12358 Coit Road, PMB #317
Dallas, TX 75251-2308

Please rush me ___ copies of *How to Dump Your Wife* @ $19.95 U.S.

= $ _____

Please rush me ___ copies of *How to Dump Your Wife* on Audio CD @ $24.95 U.S.

= $ _____

Please rush me my **FREE** gift worth $75.00 U.S. to this email: _____

= ~~$75.00~~ *FREE!*
(no shipping fee)

Postage & Handling ____ items @ $5.00 U.S./$10.00 International for first item
($2.00 per each additional item)   = $ _____

RUSH Delivery ____ Items @ $15.00 U.S./$30.00 International for first item
($5.00 per each additional item)   = $ _____

Subtotal of merchandise = $ _____

Texas Residents ONLY: Add 8.25% tax to your order
(simply multiply *SUBTOTAL* x 1.0825).   = $ _____

TOTAL = $ _____

NOTE: YOUR ORDER WILL BE SHIPPED IN PLAIN WRAPPING FROM "KAM."
WE WILL NOT SHARE YOUR INFORMATION WITH ANY PARTY.
WE WILL NOT MAIL OTHER INFORMATION OF ANY KIND TO THE ADDRESS YOU PROVIDE

Ship to (Name): _____

Address: _____

_____

City: _____ State/Province: ____ Country: ____ Zip/P.C.: _____

Phone: _____ Fax: _____

Email: _____

Method of Payment:
☐ Check – Please make payable to KAM and mail to the address shown above.
Charge to: ☐ Mastercard ☐ Visa ☐ American Express ☐ Discover
Name on Card: _____

Card Number: _____ Expiration: _____

- 146 -

ATTENTION PARENTS:

Does your son or daughter have the right skills to survive away from home in a sink-or-swim college environment? Or will they wind up right back on your couch like the **27% of young people 18-35 who still live at home,** unable to make it on their own?

HELP YOUR STUDENT ACHIEVE A'S IN COLLEGE NOW!

"Send your son or daughter to college with a PROVEN success toolbox they won't get anywhere else and be <u>confident</u> your family's college investment will pay off... **AND have employers fighting over them when they graduate!"**

IT'S NOT TOO LATE...

Whether he is a college freshman just starting out – or a senior seeking to boost her G.P.A. to the next level – this revolutionary program will make a major impact on your student's academic and professional career...

To order visit **www.kickassincollege.com**
or call 877-MY-COOL BOOK

For your FREE gift worth $49.95
send an email to **gift@kickassincollege.com**

KICK ASS IN COLLEGE

(Bulk Discounts Available)
To order please visit **www.kickassmedia.com**
<u>or</u> call us toll-free at 1-877-MY COOL BOOK
<u>or</u> Fax the order form below to: 1-877-692-7441
<u>or</u> Mail this order form to the address below:

KickAssMedia
12358 Coit Road, PMB#317
Dallas,TX 75251-2308

- -

Please rush me___ copies of *Kick Ass in College* @ $16.95 U.S.

= $ _____

Please rush me___ copies of *Kick Ass in College* on Audio CD @ $24.95 U.S.

= $ _____

Please rush me my **FREE** gift worth $49.95 U.S. to this email: _____
= $49.95 **FREE!**
(no shipping fee)
Postage & Handling___ items @ $5.00 U.S./$10.00 International for first item
($2.00 per each add'l item)
for **RUSH** delivery___ items @ $15.00 U.S./$30.00 International for first item
($5.00 per each add'l item)

= $ _____

Subtotal of merchandise = $ _____
Texas Residents: Add 8.25% tax to your order
(simply multiply SUBTOTAL x 1.0825) = $ _____

TOTAL= $ _____

Privacy notice: we will not share your information with any party.

Ship to (Name): _____

Address: _____

City: _____ State/Province: _____

Country: _____ Zip/P.C.: _____

Phone: _____ Fax: _____ Email: _____

Method of Payment:
☐ Check–Please make payable to KAM and mail to the address shown above.
Charge to: ☐ Mastercard ☐ Visa ☐ American Express ☐ Discover

Name on Card: _____

Card Number: _____ Expiration:_____

How to
DUMP
Your Wife

ACTION ITEMS

How to
DUMP
Your Wife

ACTION ITEMS

Living the Spiritually
Balanced Life

Other books by Ray S. Anderson

Minding God's Business
Theology, Death and Dying
Christians Who Counsel
The Gospel according to Judas
Ministry on the Fire Line
Don't Give Up on Me, I'm Not Finished Yet
*Self Care: A Theology of Personal Empowerment and
    Spiritual Healing*
*Everything That Makes Me Unhappy I Learned as a
    Child*
Unspoken Wisdom: Truths My Father Taught Me
The Soul of Ministry: Forming Leaders for God's People